"What made top-grossing films like *Au...* *Ferris Bueller's Day Off* so successful? I ... Voytilla and Petri explain the structure of ... how the films' writers put these principles to work."

— Melanie Rigney
Editor, *Writer's Digest Magazine*

"Writing for Hollywood is easy, selling to Hollywood is hard, and comedy is hardest of all; this book illustrates that dynamically."

— Skip Press
Author, *The Complete Idiot's Guide to Screenwriting*

"A rousing round of applause for Voytilla and Petri. They have successfully cut open the drum of film humor and let us see what all the noise is about. A classic repository of the whys and wherefores of motion picture comedy."

— Gloria Stern
Author, *Do the Write Thing: Making the Transition to Professional*
Literary consultant, Lecturer

MICHAEL WIESE PRODUCTIONS
www.mwp.com

Since 1981, Michael Wiese Productions has been dedicated to providing novice and seasoned filmmakers with vital information on all aspects of filmmaking and videomaking. We have published more than 60 books, used in over 500 film schools worldwide.

Our authors are successful industry professionals — they believe that the more knowledge and experience they share with others, the more high-quality films will be made. That's why they spend countless hours writing about the hard stuff: budgeting, financing, directing, marketing, and distribution. Many of our authors, including myself, are often invited to conduct filmmaking seminars around the world.

We truly hope that our publications, seminars, and consulting services will empower you to create enduring films that will last for generations to come.

We're here to help. Let us hear from you.

Sincerely,

Michael Wiese
Publisher, Filmmaker

WRITING THE COMEDY FILM

MAKE 'EM LAUGH

STUART VOYTILLA & SCOTT PETRI

Published by Michael Wiese Productions
11288 Ventura Blvd., Suite 621
Studio City, CA 91604
tel. (818) 379-8799
fax (818) 986-3408
mw@mwp.com
www.mwp.com

Cover Design: Art Hotel
Book layout: Gina Mansfield
Editor: Blake Snyder

Printed by McNaughton & Gunn, Inc., Saline, Michigan
Manufactured in the United States of America

©2003 Stuart Voytilla & Scott Petri

Library of Congress Cataloging-in-Publication Data

Voytilla, Stuart, 1959-
  Writing the comedy film : make 'em laugh / Stuart Voytilla, Scott Petri.
    p. cm.
  ISBN 0-941188-41-8
  1. Comedy films--History and criticism. 2. Motion picture
authorship. I. Petri, Scott, 1967- II. Title.
  PN1995.9.C55 V69 2003
  808'3--dc21

                                                    2002154211

TABLE OF CONTENTS

To Mom and Dad

— S.V.

INTRODUCTION

SIT DOWN,
SHUT UP,
AND SPLIT A GUT

What do *Home Alone, Shrek, How the Grinch Stole Christmas, Ghostbusters, Beverly Hills Cop, Rush Hour 2, Mrs. Doubtfire, Austin Powers, Toy Story,* and *Monsters, Inc.* all have in common?

No, they're not examples of huge conglomerates picking the pockets of the easily amused. What are you, some sort of NPR snob?

If you keep up with the entertainment industry, you know that the above titles are on the list of the Top 50 highest-grossing movies in U.S. history. Yes, eleven of these blockbusters are comedies. In fact, more than twenty percent of the movies produced every year are comedies. Why? Because people go to the movies to escape reality. They want to be entertained. Laughter takes their minds off their troubles.

Nothing generates positive word-of-mouth faster than laughter. People will recite the funniest lines at school or over the water cooler. They will tell their friends how funny a movie is, and urge them to go. In short, good comedies are the easiest films to market.

Can a writer learn how to write comedy? This book does not come with an "in six weeks you, too, will have the wit of Larry Gelbart!" guarantee. However, you can become a better comedy writer by understanding the purposes of comedy — why we need to laugh. This book will be a quick and easy guide to approach writing a comedy — sort of an "Elements of Style" for the trade. It offers ways of looking at comedy and understanding the basic "mechanics" of funny. We will dissect the three sides to every joke and review the tenets of comedies that have generated big laughs. A key ingredient for successful comedy writing is a comic perspective, or the ability to see the daily struggles of our world in a unique comic light. This book will teach you how to build your own distinct comic perspective and nurture the comic potential of your stories.

We will teach you how to identify jokes that can be extended into a series of related bits or set pieces. These funny sequences will exponentially increase the commercial viability of your screenplay. No one has ever rejected a script because it was too funny. Executives won't complain if tears of laughter prevent them from finishing your screenplay. Just don't make them snort Fiji Water out their nose and stain their Armani. In all seriousness, if you can make a reader laugh out loud on the first page of a screenplay, odds are you've got a sale on your hands. The hard part is putting a great joke on the next page — and on the next hundred pages — and making sure those jokes come from character and move your story forward. If you can do that, you can make a good living in this business. If not, we hear refrigeration repair pays well.

We will identify the major genres of comedy and talk about what makes them so effective. In order to exploit the popularity of comedies, the movie industry has blended them into sub-genres, so there are now literally dozens of types of comedies. Primarily, we will concentrate on the fish-out-of-water comedy, romantic comedy, sports comedy, crime/caper comedy, military comedy, teen comedy, ensemble comedy, as well as farce, satire, parody, and mockumentary. You will learn that these genres are nothing more than simple strategies for storytelling. In time, you will think of genre as a coach's trusted playbook, containing surefire diagrams for how to triumph over a formidable complex of goals, obstacles, and set pieces.

By using Joseph Campbell's *Hero's Journey* paradigm, we gain insight into the recurring patterns of these comic sub-genres. Each has its own set of guidelines. What makes a teen comedy different from a farce? We'll show you how each has different types of heroes, goals, antagonists, obstacles, and journeys. (Since we refer to this mythic terminology throughout the book, we've included a quick-and-dirty refresher in the Appendix.) This type of analysis additionally allows us to better understand the audience expectations that are built into specific sub-genres. By appreciating audience expectations, a writer can reel an audience in and then sucker punch them with surprising comic vision. Yes, you can break guidelines and defy structure. But the comic writer benefits from understanding these structural patterns and audience expectations in order to know <u>what</u> rules to break and <u>when</u> to break them. Oh, and you better be #@$%ing funny.

Hopefully, this book will make you do some reflection on your own comic soul. Does your funny bone speak with the satirical wit of Alexander Payne or the broad slap and tickle of the Farrelly Brothers? Do you want to intelligently slay the sacred cows our society falsely worships? Or do you prefer wild slapstick? Whatever your desire, we will help transform your comic voice into a strong and powerful weapon. Before you turn the page, you must promise that you will only use these powers for good and never for evil. Promise? Mean it?

If you are a writer who is drifting through a comic screenplay, this book will help you find new ways to develop the distinct comic voice needed to finish your project. If you are a new writer just thinking about starting a screenplay, this book will serve as a handy guide in determining which genre you are suited for. Readers can start from page one and read straight through for a comprehensive comedy primer, or simply reference the genre that's important to you and dive back into your own project with renewed insight. Our focus is on comedy films, with most of our examples pulled from cinema. But knowing these comic techniques will help you be a better comic writer regardless of what you write: sit-coms, greeting cards, children's humor, commercials, stand-up comedy, or even if you are trying to spice up the comic relief in a romance book or action film. This book is written to all of you. Turn the page and get ready to make 'em laugh.

THE **1**
COMIC PERSPECTIVE:
HOW TO DEVELOP
A COMIC VOICE

Comedy offers a unique perspective of our world. We call this the **comic perspective**. There are two distinct ways to look at comic perspective:

- The comic perspective of the writer, director, or feature comic
- The approach to the subject or story

Comic perspective is the unique comic point of view of a comic artist. The way a writer, director, or performer spins a story to look at it from an unusual viewpoint. In this sense, style and voice are synonymous. Theme and variation are two ways to identify and define a specific comic point of view. A piece could be satirical, ironic, bitter, optimistic, positive, negative, or naive depending on who is telling the tale.

Later in the chapter, we'll look at how two variations on a similar theme played out with different comic voices. First, let's look at some different styles.

THE WRITER'S PERSPECTIVE: KEVIN SMITH VS. WOODY ALLEN

Kevin Smith is a writer/director from New Jersey. Since his debut film, *Clerks*, he's given us *Chasing Amy*, *Mall Rats*, *Dogma*, *Jay and Silent Bob*

Strike Back, and *Jersey Girl*. One might say Mr. Smith represents Jersey well. He's polluted, twisted, and dirty — God love him. No doubt, the Garden State is proud. *Clerks* was released in 1994 by Miramax. The movie was made for $27,000 and grossed over $3 million in the United States. The story offers viewers a glimpse into the over-the-counter culture and centers on two slackers stuck in miserable, dead-end jobs. Dante has been called into work on his day off and is torn between two girlfriends. In this exchange, he and his current girlfriend discuss past relationships.

```
INT. CONVENIENCE STORE - DAY

Dante  and  Veronica  are  slumped  on  the  floor,
behind the counter.

                    DANTE
          How many dicks have you sucked?!

                    VERONICA
          Let it go...

                    DANTE
          HOW MANY?

                    VERONICA
          All right! Shut up a second and
          I'll tell you! Jesus! I didn't
          freak like this when you told me
          how many girls you fucked.

                    DANTE
          This is different. This is important.
          How many?!

She  counts  silently,  using  fingers  as  marks.
```

Dante waits on a customer in the interim.
Veronica stops counting.

                    DANTE
          Well...?

                    VERONICA
               (half-mumbled)
          Something like thirty-six.

                    DANTE
     WHAT? SOMETHING LIKE THIRTY-SIX?

                    VERONICA
     Lower your voice!

                    DANTE
     What the hell is that anyway,
     "something like thirty-six?" Does
     that include me?

                    VERONICA
     Um. Thirty-seven.

                    DANTE
     I'M THIRTY-SEVEN?

Woody Allen uses a sophisticated New York intellectual style humor. He also has a distinctly neurotic, insecure voice which can be referenced in *Annie Hall*. In this scene, protagonist Alvy Singer tries to cajole his girlfriend, Annie Hall, into sex.

INT. BEDROOM - NIGHT

Annie is sitting up in bed reading.

                    ALVY
               (Off screen)
     Boy, those guys in the French Resistance
     were really brave, you know? Got to listen
     to Maurice Chevalier sing so much.

                    ANNIE
     M'm, I don't know, sometimes I ask myself
     how I'd stand up under torture.

                    ALVY
               (Off screen)
     You? You kiddin'?
               (He moves into the frame, lying across
               the bed to touch Annie, who makes a
               face)
     If the Gestapo would take away your
     Bloomingdale's charge card, you'd tell 'em
     everything.

                    ANNIE
     That movie makes me feel guilty.

                    ALVY
     Yeah, 'cause it's supposed to.

He starts kissing Annie's arm. She gets annoyed
and continues to read.

                    ANNIE
     Alvy, I ...

                    ALVY
     What-what-what-what's the matter?

4

```
                    ANNIE
      I-you know, I don't wanna.

                    ALVY
            (Overlapping Annie, reacting)
      What-what-I don't... It's not natural!
      We're sleeping in a bed together.  You
      know, it's been a long time.

                    ANNIE
      I know, well, it's just that-you know, I
      mean, I-I-I-I gotta sing tomorrow night,
      so I have to rest my voice.

                    ALVY
            (Overlapping Annie again)
      It's always some kind of an excuse.  It's-
      You know, you used to think that I was
      very sexy.  What... When we first started
      going out, we had sex constantly... We're-
      we're probably listed in the Guinness Book
      of World Records.

                    ANNIE
            (Patting Alvy's hand solicitously)
      I know.  Well, Alvy, it'll pass, it'll
      pass, it's just that I'm going through a
      phase, that's all.

                    ALVY
      M'm.
```

Here we have two similar scenes featuring characters dealing with their girlfriends. However, the voices are distinctly different. Kevin Smith's humor is raunchy and raw, bordering on the obscene.

However, it accurately reflects the profanity-filled lives of working class teens. His voice has an honesty and strength that cannot be denied. In contrasting angst, Woody Allen's Alvy is an intellectual who overanalyzes everything and is frankly a little irritating. Who else would use references to the French Resistance to seduce his mate? Each comic has created material that has resonated with mass audiences. Each filmmaker has attracted his own legion of fans. These fans will remain loyal because they are drawn to the individual's comic perspective. However, you won't find these fans at the same parties.

THE DIRECTOR'S PERSPECTIVE: JOHN HUGHES VS. TOM SHADYAC

Ferris Bueller's Day Off, *The Breakfast Club*, *Sixteen Candles*, *Planes, Trains and Automobiles*, and *Weird Science* were all directed by John Hughes. Many of Hughes' earlier successes were due to his ability to speak to, and for, teenagers. His other strength is his gift for slapstick comedy, which can be seen in his screenwriting contributions to *Flubber*, *Beethoven*, *Home Alone*, *National Lampoon's Christmas Vacation*, and *Mr. Mom*. We will explore his unique comic voice later when we analyze *Flubber*. Although he'll probably never win an Oscar (comedians never get any respect — just ask Rodney Dangerfield), John Hughes has been the pre-eminent comic director and writer of his generation. His work has influenced thousands of young filmmakers.

Tom Shadyac directed three of the biggest comedies of the 1990s: *Ace Ventura: Pet Detective*, *The Nutty Professor*, and *Liar Liar*. These movies are all characterized by low-brow, bodily-function-oriented humor — which explains why Jim Carrey stars in two of them. In *The Nutty Professor*, Shadyac was able to give Eddie Murphy freedom to tap into his body's natural comic reservoir as well. After directing two of today's top comic stars to box office gold, Shadyac will continue his work as an outstanding comic director in the years to come.

FEATURED COMIC'S PERSPECTIVE: DENNIS MILLER VS.
CHRIS ROCK

Dennis Miller uses his cynical voice to comment on ways our society
has gone awry. In a collection of his HBO monologues entitled
Ranting Again, Dennis sounds off on ethnicity in America:

> "Bottom line. America is a polyglot, bastardized
> culture. It's been settled by wave after wave of
> immigrants who assimilated and became part of the
> establishment so that they could look down their
> noses at the next wave of immigrants. Therein lies
> the paradox of this great land of ours. Freedom of
> belief also means freedom to make fun of the 7-
> Eleven guy's sandals, all right?"[1]

Chris Rock speaks with a similar cynical voice, but uses an angry point of
view, cutting through political correctness and exposing the bitter truth
about what really represses the African-American underclass. In his
HBO special, *Bigger and Blacker*, the bad boy of comedy serves up brutal
opinions about racism, gun control, police brutality, and single parents:

> "There's racism everywhere. Who's the maddest
> people? White people. White man thinks he's losing
> the country. Shut up! White people ain't losing shit.
> If you losing, who's winning? It ain't us. Have you
> driven around? There ain't a white man in this room
> that would change places with me. And I'm rich!
> That's how good it is to be white. There's a white,
> one-legged busboy in here right now that won't
> change places with my black ass!"

Stand-up comics need to develop a very strong point of view in order
to build an act. Often successful acts lead to sit-com and/or movie

---

[1] *Ranting Again* by Dennis Miller, © 1998, Doubleday

stardom. Bill Cosby was the family man. Roseanne Barr was the lazy, disgruntled housewife. Tim Allen was the tool man.

STORY'S OR THEME'S PERSPECTIVE: *FLUBBER* VS. *THE NUTTY PROFESSOR*

Comic perspective is but a variable in the comedic formula. When variations on a theme or story premise are mixed with a strong comedic perspective, look out. You've got lightning in a bottle.

Pretty much any story can be redone in a comedic way. For instance, a story based on mother and son relationships can range from *Psycho* to *Throw Momma from the Train*. Think of the endless comic variations on this theme: *Spanking the Monkey*, *Mother*, *Divine Secrets of the Ya-Ya Sisterhood*. It's all in the approach and storyteller's comic vision: one's unique perspective of the story's theme, world, and its characters. Whenever a unique comic perspective is stamped on material, it revitalizes the genre and makes it feel new again. You may not be able to teach an old dog new tricks, but you can get an audience to see an old story, if you add a new twist.

Both *Flubber* (1997) and *The Nutty Professor* (1996) are remakes, or riffs on classic films, respectively *The Absent-Minded Professor* (1961) and *The Nutty Professor* (1963) . They are very similar in theme and tone; however, they each employ a distinct comic voice influenced by the filmmakers, and by each film's featured actor: Robin Williams and Eddie Murphy. Each movie offers a similar story: a brilliant scientist's attempt to use an experiment to save his college, his career, and his romance. *Flubber's* Professor Brainard (Robin Williams) discovers Flubber, a substance with the power to magnify energy. In *The Nutty Professor*, Sherman Klump (Eddie Murphy) discovers a secret formula for genetic restructuring.

Brainard uses his discovery to manipulate objects, including his car and the shoes on the school's basketball team. And the Flubber is used

8

against the bad guys who try to steal it from Brainard. Klump uses his experiment for deeper, personal stakes. He transforms from the painfully shy, grossly fat Klump to overconfident, slim-and-trim Buddy Love. This distinction helps distinguish the primary type of comedy used in each film. *Flubber* has a stronger slapstick feel. Set pieces and sight gags rely upon characters coping with the rubbery Flubber substance and powerful Flubber-laced objects. Although *The Nutty Professor* dishes out its share of physical comedy, in contrast, it relies on the comedy of embarrassment. Sherman Klump is the gargantuan butt of the majority of verbal and physical jokes. This effectively divides our vicarious or empathetic eye as moments of laughing at fat Klump can quickly be turned to moments of feeling his pain. The film taps Murphy's exceptional skills at manipulating audience emotions. His prowess at impersonation is also showcased. He becomes every elder member of the Klump family. Each character has a strong voice, and gets laughs in their own right — if you enjoy bathroom humor. They're fat; they fart and insult each other.

A film's comic perspective can be established in the opening moments of the story, setting up the rules of the new world and hooking the audience. Each movie opens in a way that reveals its comic tone. *Flubber* opens with a Rube Goldberg set-up of machines. These are necessary for Brainard, who is absent-minded enough to forget his own wedding. Everything is clever and classy and logical. We know we are gearing up for a wild, slapstick ride. *The Nutty Professor* opens with Sherman watching a fitness video parody and trying to cram his fat body into tight clothes. We get the sense that there will be a lot of personal, embarrassing humor involving body parts and, from what Sherman is eating, perhaps some flatulence.

From a deeper story level, comic perspective can define a character. In our two sample films, each character sees the world from his unique comic viewpoint influenced by his comic flaws. Brainard is absent-minded. He's already forgotten his wedding ceremony twice, and relies on an interactive personal robot, Weebo, to keep his appointments. At stake on the personal level are his career and his relationship with his fiancée. Sherman Klump's comic flaw is his weight. Not just rotund, Klump is a lovable four-hundred pounds. He resorts to eating in order to deal with anxiety, which is in abundance. Painfully shy and bumbling, Klump needs research funds to save his position. And he's fallen for a beautiful graduate student, Carla Purty (Jada Pinkett). His dream is to shed the pounds to win Carla's heart. These unique comic perspectives help define the character and determine his actions within the story's world.

Both Brainard and Klump initially try to overcome their comic flaws, but by the end of the story learn to accept themselves for who they are. And their respective romantic interests accept and celebrate their uniqueness as well. This is both stories' common theme.

By looking at these two films, we can see that stories with similar story lines and themes can be distinctive comedies as determined by the performers, the filmmakers, the execution of the story, and the style of comedy used. All combine to form the story's comic perspective.

By now, you should have a good idea what comic perspective is — it's the way you look at the world. Here are some exercises to help you see your own comic perspective.

EXERCISES:

1. Who are your favorite comedians or comediennes? Do you have a favorite comedy writer? Comedy director? How would you describe their comic perspective?

2. What are your all-time favorite comedies? Think hard about this. Taste in comedy can change with age. Go ahead, write them down. These will help you to better understand your own comic point of view. Is there any consistency to these titles? Are they all the same type or style of comedy? Is the same actor in one or more of them? If so, this actor speaks to your comic voice. Think about his/her persona. What do you like about it? What do you dislike about it?

3. Using your list of favorite comedies, how would you describe the type of comedy that you enjoy most as an audience member? Slapstick, gross-out humor, romantic comedy? Is it built around a particular type of situation? Is it generated by a particular artist (i.e., W.C. Fields, the Marx Brothers, Steve Martin, or Meg Ryan)?

4. Try putting your unique comic spin on a tried-and-true dramatic story. Could *Casablanca* be retold if it was a love triangle involving a beautiful coed and two mattress salesmen? *"If you don't buy the Posturepedic, you'll regret it. Maybe not today, maybe not tomorrow, but soon and for the rest of your life on your back." "What about us, Rick?" "We'll always have Sealy."* Think about changing the perspective of some of your supporting characters. Instead of a clichéd cop who drinks too much, how about a cop who does pottery? Robert DeNiro played one in *Showtime* to considerable comedic effect.

5. Take each of the following situations and see them first from a serious perspective:
- A woman standing in an unemployment line.
- A crime scene of a man who has been killed.
- A corporate meeting.
- A chance meeting of two soul mates.
- A senior citizen making a purchase at a drug store.

Now look at the same situations from a comic perspective:
- A woman standing in an unemployment line. She scratches off a lottery ticket and becomes a winner.
- A crime scene of a man who was bludgeoned by a pot roast.
- A corporate meeting for snack manufacturer, Ding-Dong.
- A chance meeting of two suicidal people arriving at lover's leap.
- A senior citizen buying condoms at a drug store.

6. See the following premises for Shakespearean tragedies in a comic light:
- Two lovers separated by family differences, but are determined to be together.
- A man's obsession to claim the kingdom with his power-hungry wife at his side.
- A young man is haunted by the ghost of his father and driven to get revenge against his father's murderer.

7. What are the top five funniest cinematic moments that you can remember? Why were they funny to you?

8. Choose someone you know very well and find a personality trait that can be exaggerated. Can you turn this quirk into a comic perspective? Of course you can. Turn a point of view into an obsession and you've created a memorable character.

Chatty mother-in-law? Cheap accountant? Fastidious dresser? Everything is brimming over with comic potential. Pick up the ball and run with it. Just don't run with scissors.

9. What is the most humiliating moment from your childhood? Using age as a distancing technique, can you now see the humor of that moment? What if you were watching it happen to someone else? Don't pick an event that you haven't already come to grips with.

10. Start to twist the everyday situations of ordinary life into bits that fit your comic perspective. How would a nervous Nelly answer the phone? Would they hide from it or be scared by the ring? How does an angry person do the dishes? Unsuccessfully, we would imagine. But wouldn't it be funny if a brute smashed all the dishes in the house and had to serve dinner in pots and pans? How does a paranoid person answer the door? How do they treat the Christian Scientists at the door? *"My mother sent you here, didn't she?! Damn her! She's always praying for my salvation."*

11. How would you describe your comic perspective?

12. What can you do to nurture it? Or pervert it? Extremes are good when it comes to comedy. Laughter is hardly ever subtle.

HOW 2
COMEDY WORKS:
THE PHYSICS OF FUNNY

In order to better grasp how comedy works, why we laugh, we're going to look at comedy from a mechanical level. This chapter will focus on the physical properties of comedy as we explore the importance of:

- Comic Distance
- Surprise and Suspense
- The Magic Three

COMIC DISTANCE

The fundamental mechanic of comedy is **comic distance**, the ability to separate ourselves from an event in order to laugh at it. Mel Brooks has the best definition of comic distance. It has been quoted many times, by many humorists, explaining why we laugh at pain. Brooks said, "I cut my finger, that's tragedy. If you fall down a sewer, that's comedy." [2]

By understanding comic distance, the comic writer wields a powerful prism through which to look at comedy in two fundamental ways:

- We can *maintain* comic distance in order to allow the audience to laugh at the situation on screen. We want to distance the audience from the pain.

---

[2] *Funny Business: The Craft of Writing Comedy* by Sol Saks, © 1985 Lone Eagle Publishing

15

- We can *break* the comic distance when we want the audience to identify or empathize with the character on screen. In other words, we want the audience to feel the pain.

THE NEED TO MAINTAIN COMIC DISTANCE

Comic distance is the ability to stand back — distance ourselves vicariously — so that we can laugh at the situation. We watch as voyeurs and feel safe that we can laugh without consequence. It is true that comedy is pain. And if we have the right amount of distance, we heartily laugh at the misfortunes of others. If it's too close to the bone, we wince and the laughter becomes an Owww! We laugh when Ben Stiller gets caught in his zipper in *There's Something About Mary*, but if that had happened to us in real life would we still be laughing?

How do we maintain comic distance? The visual presentation of the character can be the simplest way. Why do we laugh at circus clowns? Their presentation gives us permission. Their outrageous make-up and clothes, and slapstick antics, tell children of all ages it's okay to laugh.

The use of exaggerated costumes, whether it be masks or false body parts, has been a tradition of comic presentation reaching back to Greek and Roman comedies. We often see characters wearing stock masks and phalluses to establish comic distance, again giving us permission to laugh at whatever may happen to them. The silent film clowns — Charlie Chaplin, Buster Keaton, Harold Lloyd — used costumes and make-up to maintain this comic distance, giving the audience permission to laugh at their mishaps.

Outrageous actions and events can also help to maintain comic distance. Like the tradition of the circus clown that relies on roustabout physical humor, comic distance is extremely important to appreciate slapstick and other physical comedy. The tradition of grand Mack Sennett slapstick oftentimes had bodies hurled as if they were physical objects. Like watching a Road Runner or Tom and Jerry cartoon, we could feel free to laugh at this comic pain because it was exaggerated and unreal. The Keystone Cops may get sandwiched between two passing cable cars, but we know they will live to chase again.

Maintaining comic distance is as important in the stories we tell today. Comedy's outrageous tendency helps strengthen this distance. In Disney's *The Emperor's New Groove*, Emperor Kuzco is turned into a llama. Sure we can feel for the selfish brat, but he's a llama.

In the remake of the aforementioned *Nutty Professor*, Sherman Klump is not just overweight, but tips the scales at four-hundred pounds.

Developing a character's comic flaw can help establish this distance. The comic flaw defines how a character uniquely sees the world. Although we see this flaw as defining a character that isn't perfect, the outrageousness of the flaw helps maintain the comic distance. The audience says, "He's not perfect, like me" but distance is maintained by the extreme nature of the comic flaw, "I'm not perfect, but I'm certainly not that bad!" The comic flaw can be physical: Cyrano's nose in *Cyrano de Bergerac* and Steve Martin's update, *Roxanne*; Inspector Clouseau's bumbling in the Pink Panther series. It can be an attitude: Michael Dorsey's chauvinism and holier-than-thou perfectionism (*Tootsie*), Brainard's absent-mindedness (*Flubber*), or Amélie's innocence in *Amélie*. The flaw can be a gift or talent: the amazing lying skills of attorney Fletcher Reede (Jim Carrey) in *Liar Liar*.

But distancing the audience from the event isn't enough to create a satisfying comic story.

THE NEED TO BREAK COMIC DISTANCE

Breaking comic distance can help create instant identification with a character. We can feel the pain of the character and thus identify and root for the character on the journey.

17

The first comic shorts were usually delegated to the warm-up for a feature drama or melodrama. But as D.W. Griffith had fought to make feature-length silent films, so did comic filmmakers try to gain respect for comedy and push the length of comic stories. To make the comic story more sophisticated, characters needed more depth. The key was to break comic distance, giving the audience opportunities to identify with characters while laughing at their antics.

Two important filmmakers that contributed to this dual use of comic distance were Buster Keaton and Charlie Chaplin. The two had different styles of acting and storytelling, but both styles allowed the audience to laugh *while also identifying with character*.

Buster Keaton usually places his stoic character in extreme situations where he must stand up to a heroic task — a heroic journey in its classic sense. In *Sherlock Jr.*, he must find the real thief when he's accused of stealing his future father-in-law's watch. In *The General*, Buster plays a railroad engineer in the South during the Civil War who must retrieve his second love (the train) from a band of Union Soldiers who have taken it. Both are truly heroic stories. But he remains deadpan throughout, allowing the audience to provide the emotions he must be feeling. And as director, Keaton's preference for medium and long shots enhance this dual use of comic distance. We watch Keaton in his slapstick environment at a physical distance from us, as if he were on stage. Yet, we are also identifying with Keaton's hero. Take a look at any of Keaton's classics, and you'll find yourself empathizing with him, giving him the "appropriate" emotions concerning his situation, even though he remains "The Great Stoneface" throughout.

In contrast, Charlie Chaplin distances us, like many of the silent clowns, with his costume and slapstick antics. But Chaplin entrances our vicarious eye with his anti-heroic Tramp's ability to thwart authority. Additionally he uses a powerful film technique: the close-up.

18

Chaplin's Little Tramp is a trickster anti-hero, the lowly clown that uses wit and brawn to stand up to bullies and characters representing the establishment (cops, bosses, high society). His are not pure heroic journey tales, but stories of the Everyman doing his best to survive. Chaplin also uses the close-up to allow the audience to get into Chaplin's head and heart and experience what the Tramp is feeling. We don't have the stoic face of Keaton, but we have a character's subtle reactions to situation.

Each technique effectively breaks down comic distance, giving us a character with whom we can empathize and invest screen time, vicariously living their journey.

Other filmmakers and screen comedians use other techniques to break comic distance. W.C. Fields is the comic hero as hapless victim. His victimization tugs at our empathy. His characters repeatedly receive the wrath of everyone in authority, until we have to feel for the guy.

In the brilliant *Annie Hall*, Woody Allen uses several film and storytelling techniques to break comic distance and allow us to see the world through Alvy Singer's eyes. Allen uses direct address, animation, and interaction with his past experiences to help us get into this character's mind and heart.

In *Bridget Jones's Diary*, Bridget confesses her deepest secrets in her diary — which are revealed as voice-over narration. Again, a technique that fuels our identification with Bridget Jones.

The power of maintaining and breaking comic distance is demonstrated in an important scene from the remake of *The Nutty Professor* starring Eddie Murphy. The scene takes place in a comedy club. At the top of the sequence he leads his dream date to their front row seats, his huge ass pushing customers over, toppling their drinks and tables. We're allowed to laugh at his gargantuan size — comic distance is maintained. But in the next few moments, Klump becomes the butt of a stand-up comic's merciless assault. We feel his pain as the comic rips into him. In mere seconds, we witness the total destruction of Sherman's dignity.

The filmmakers use this scene to shatter the comic distance between Sherman and the audience. It creates an instant bond with the character. Yes, Sherman was the buffoon with the big ass that we laughed at just a few moments ago, but now we identify with him completely. We're behind him 100% as he proceeds to the next stage of his journey. The audience understands why Sherman will become a human guinea pig to test his body transformation experiment. Further, we're rooting for him.

SURPRISE AND SUSPENSE

No, this isn't a book on writing thrillers; however, comedy has an important kinship with the thriller. Both genres rely on **suspense** and **surprise** for their respective audience payoffs. In the thriller, the payoff is fear and terror. In comedy, laughter. Additionally, we'll see how surprise and suspense allow us to better understand the mechanics of any joke. But what are suspense and surprise?

SUSPENSE IS INEVITABILITY

Suspense is the audience's anticipation of something that is bound to happen. The audience is placed in a position where they know more than the characters on screen. Because the audience is "in the know," they're feeling an inevitability that something will happen. An element of suspense can be established by the simple appearance of an item (prop) or person. Paraphrasing the great playwright Anton Chekhov, if you show a gun on stage in Act One, it better go off by Act Three. That is suspense and inevitability. But a gun sounds pretty serious. How does this apply to comedy?

In *Ferris Bueller's Day Off*, our trickster hero, Ferris, takes a day off from school with the inner goal of building his best friend Cameron's self-esteem. To take this journey, Ferris offers the prized possession of Cameron's materialistic father — a red Ferrari that took three years to rebuild (even more important in his materialistic dad's world than Cameron himself). What's the element of inevitability or suspense from this introduction? At some point we know the car will be totaled.

Later in the "Tenets of Laughter," (Chapter Three), we'll discover that delusion or deception is a common successful element in comedy. The hero must create some element of deception to get what he or she is after. In gender-bending stories like *Tootsie, Some Like It Hot,* or *Victor/Victoria*, the deception is the cross-dressing disguise. The element of inevitability that is established in the back of our minds is when the disguise will be revealed. As the hero's disguise becomes more difficult to maintain because of growing complications, the suspense is heightened and the discovery of the deception becomes even more inevitable.

We must stress that these examples show story elements that are known by the audience. That's why they are considered elements of suspense. The element has been sufficiently established to the audience, as well as the stakes involved if the ticking clock indeed goes off. If the Ferrari is destroyed, we believe, as does Cameron, that he'll be killed by his dad. If, in *Tootsie*, Michael's disguise as Dorothy is revealed, he'll lose his successful job as a soap star. Other characters may not know it, but we do. The audience is in the know. If we've crafted our comedy successfully, the final pay-off, i.e., the destruction of the Ferrari and the dropping of the disguise, will be great comic moments.

SURPRISE IS THE UNEXPECTED

Surprise is something that happens that was unexpected by the audience. The characters <u>may</u> be aware of the element, but the

21

audience isn't. Whatever happens is a surprise. Yes, the smart audience member, well-nurtured with comic gags and plots, may guess the surprise, but the comic writer seeks to craft the surprise element so that the audience isn't aware of it. For the surprise is what will yield the laughter.

As successful comedy does, suspense and surprise can be used to deceive the audience into believing certain expectations that don't pay off. Instead they are reversed, offering surprise and laughter.

Let's look at a classic physical gag to show how this works. The moment is from Buster Keaton's short *One Week* (1920). In the story, Buster has just married, much to the disgust of a rival for his bride's hand. Buster receives a pre-fabricated house, which was delivered in numbered crates. The rival villain switches the numbers around without the newlyweds' knowledge (but the audience is in the know, setting up an element of suspense — "Will the house be built?"). With determination, Buster and his bride make the house per these new instructions. The odd configuration of the house is a comic payoff. But things get worse for our couple. After a whirlwind housewarming, they are told that they've placed their house on the wrong lot and they'll have to move it across the railroad tracks to the right lot.

Alas, they get the house stuck on the railroad tracks just as a train is coming (suspense). We, (the audience), see the approaching train, but what we don't realize is that it's on the far track. It barely misses the house (surprise), and we laugh at the last-second averted destruction. Buster and his bride are also relieved — until another train coming from the opposite direction (and from off-screen) plows through the house, turning it to tinder. (A surprise topper that leaves us laughing.) Yes, we feel for Buster's loss, but we also laugh that the inevitability played out as anticipated, *but in a manner that wasn't anticipated*. And we laugh at the total destruction of a train plowing through the house. Of course this type of reversal has been re-treaded over and over again in numerous gags and storylines. Yet it is still fresh in the deft directorial hands of this comic genius.

22

Let's see this again with new dressing from Disney's *The Emperor's New Groove* (2000). The selfish brat, Emperor Kuzco, has been drugged by his nemesis, his ex-administrator, Yzma. Although she hoped to off him, instead her bumbling assistant, Kronk, messed up the potion and the Emperor has been turned into a llama. Now Kuzco has to fend for himself in the Andean wilds. Before his transformation, Kuzco is so selfish that he wants to level a hilltop village to begin construction of his private estate — Kuzcotopia! He's explained his plan to the village spokesman, a farmer and llama herder, Pancha. One overall element of suspense is established. Will Kusco indeed destroy the village out of selfishness or will Pancha convince him to change his mind? It's inevitable that these two contrasting characters will meet up — and the former emperor, now a talking llama, indeed ends up in the farmer's cart.

The physical gag happens while Kuzco (as llama) is stranded at the end of a precipice surrounded by hungry panthers. He has nowhere to go except falling to his death or into the mouths of panthers. However, we see the farmer swing to the rescue on a vine. What's inevitable... that he'll pluck Kuzco from the precipice. What's the element of suspense? Will he do it in time? Since the audience sees him established on the vine, the ticking clock is sufficiently set.

What happens? Pancha misses (a surprise). He's failed. We didn't expect this and we laugh. (At this point in the story, we wouldn't mind seeing Kuzco become panther bait... or at least sweat a little bit longer.) Now the panthers are ready to pounce. But the farmer is able to take the backward swing to successfully save Kuzco. The backward swing wasn't established, presenting an opportunity for surprise (he came back and completed the job). And again, the payoff is laughter. Our inevitability was fulfilled. Kuzco is saved (at least from this cliffhanger). Our fear of seeing the llama torn apart by panthers is averted, all contributing to that mysterious laughter response.

Let's use suspense and surprise to help us understand the mechanics of any joke. Humorists and comic theorists often break a joke down into two parts:

23

- The Set-up
- The Payoff or punch line

Incorporating suspense and surprise, we can see these two parts from a new perspective:

- What does the audience anticipate will happen? This is the element of suspense or inevitability (set-up).
- What actually happens? This is the surprise, the unexpected or incongruous (punch line).

Let's revisit our physical gag with Buster's house stuck on the railroad tracks. But we're going to look at it from this new perspective.

The first half of the gag:
What is anticipated? The train will smash the house.

What actually happens? The first train misses the house.

The second half of the gag:
What is anticipated? Buster and his wife have saved the house. They just have to get it off the tracks.

What actually happens? A second unexpected train plows through the house.

In order for the joke to succeed, there's a third element that needs to be accounted for: *what the audience knows*. This includes everything that the writer must include to effectively set up the joke so that the audience can "get it." This is often neglected by the comic writer and can lead to the failure of the punch line.

Again, using Buster's situation, the audience sees the first train coming. This effectively sets up the inevitability of collision. The audience doesn't realize that there are two tracks. Destruction is averted. This surprise punch line succeeds. In the gag's second half, neither audience

24

nor Buster knows about the second train. This successful surprise payoff yields destruction and laughter.

Generally, the physical gag is easier to pull off. The audience can quickly get the joke, because all of the elements of comedy are visually present on screen. The audience doesn't need to know a lot in order to appreciate the humor. From a directing point of view, this emphasizes the need to establish the elements as needed on screen in order to sufficiently set up the joke. If you look at Keaton's work, you'll appreciate the power of wide-shots in directing because we can see the actor in the middle of the environment as the physical comedy is played out. If Buster is going to have a run-in with a mop, we'll need to set up the mop. Effective set-ups of visual gags are giving the important elements sufficient screen time without overtly indicating that the element will be used.

Remember the great comic moment in *Raiders of the Lost Ark*? A satisfying comic surprise that was still effectively set up. Indy faces a duel with a giant Arab swordsman. All he has is his whip. Or does he? He takes a beat to size up his adversary (timing is indeed everything), pulls out his gun, and shoots the swordsman dead. We don't see the gun before he draws, we don't need to. Again, the laughter is in the surprise. However, the moment fits logically within the story, because as he was packing his bag, he tossed his gun into the suitcase. It was clearly, subtly established.

Verbal jokes are more tricky and we have to pay attention to what the audience knows and, even more important, be aware of what the audience doesn't know.

Comedy works on levels of deception and multiple levels of awareness. Verbal jokes thrive on these multiple levels of understanding. The comedy writer diverts the audience to believe one track of logic or thinking and surprises them with another level of meaning. Verbal jokes can be broken down using the same mechanics of surprise and suspense that we used in visual jokes.

25

What is anticipated? The first level of meaning is established.

What actually happens? The incongruous or unexpected new level of meaning forms the punch line.

What does the audience know? If the two levels of meaning are not clear in the actual telling of the joke, we have to hope and pray that that audience already has the sufficient life experience to "get the joke."

To understand this initially, recall the last time you told a joke that your audience didn't get. Remember the time you then had to take to try to <u>explain</u> the joke? Explaining after the telling doesn't give you back the laugh. And you certainly don't have the luxury of explaining your jokes on screen. However, appreciating what your audience knows, and what you must tell them prior to the jokes, can help you effectively set up your comic world. And punch up the punch line.

Let's first look at a simple children's joke:
> *Q: What time is it when an elephant sits on the fence?*
> *A: Time to get a new fence.*

What is anticipated? A designation of time is the ploy or diversion, sending the listener to the matter-of-fact level of the joke — what time (on the clock) is it?

What actually happens? The elephant destroys the fence. This unexpected payoff (surprise) reveals the second level of the joke. The physical fact that a standard fence can't support an elephant.

The success of the joke depends upon what the audience knows, which is why this is such a successful children's riddle. The knowledge of the joke is pretty accessible. Not a lot of life experience is needed to understand it. Most children have a basic understanding of time, elephants, and fences, and personal experiences with the law of gravity. You try to climb on something precarious and you'll fall.

Let's look at a bit more sophisticated child's riddle:
Q: Why is it so hard to fool a snake?
A: Because you can't pull its leg.

What is anticipated? The logical and literal level of interpretation of this riddle is the word "fool," meaning "to joke."

What actually happens? The comic payoff is the second level of "fool," meaning to "pull one's leg," and the fact that snakes don't have legs.

What does the audience know? This joke isn't so obvious to the young child. They need a bit more life experience to appreciate it. If the child led a sufficiently sheltered life and didn't know that a snake doesn't have legs, or more likely, if a child doesn't know that "to pull its leg" is a play on the word "fool," then this joke wouldn't get a reaction. It would need explanation.

If you are telling that joke to a group, then you better hope that the majority of your audience has the needed outside knowledge or life experience to appreciate the joke. Otherwise, you're going to die.

THE MAGIC THREE: ANTICIPATION AND INCONGRUITY

No physical exploration of comedy is complete without mentioning comedy's magic three. What is **the magic three**? It is a series of three repetitive events, actions, reactions, or lines of dialogue. The first and second times are the same event. But the third time gives us the payoff, reversal, or an unexpected surprise. Why is the "three" a successful gag? Surprise and suspense help us unlock the secret power of this comic technique.

The first beat of a comic three establishes the act, whatever it may be, a line of dialogue, response, or action. The audience has no true connection to its significance over the long haul. It's simply established.

The second time we see that same event or hear the line of dialogue, a pattern of repetition is established. Importantly, the repetition builds audience expectations that it will happen again.

Since the audience has now figured out the pattern, the third time should yield the same event or dialogue. Right? That's the audience's expectation. The comic payoff happens because the writer defeats audience expectation and gives them something unexpected.

Think of a child playing peekaboo. You're holding a "blankie" in front of your face. Revealed once, and a child smiles at the unexpected revelation of your face. Play it a second time with the same motion and the child giggles. And sees the pattern. "Ah-ha, this person's head will soon appear at the top of my blankie." Now, the third time, you surprise the little one, revealing your face from a different side of the blankie. Expectations have been built and the child expects the reveal — but the reveal is at an unexpected location. Suspense, surprise, laughter. This topper solicits giggling with joy. And the baby's hooked for more of this game.

Let's look at a physical and a verbal "three" in film to illustrate the mechanics we've explored. First, a simple physical "three" from the sports comedy *The Bad News Bears*.

The Bears are a bunch of misfit Little League baseball hopefuls being coached by an alcoholic, washed-up minor league pitcher now pool-cleaner, played by Walter Matthau.

The "three" shows the progressive reaction of the Bear's short (and short-tempered) shortstop missing three successive ground balls. The first time he misses the grounder, he throws down his glove in disgust. He botches the second grounder and throws down his glove in disgust again. This establishes the pattern of his reaction. If it were to happen a third time, we anticipate that he'd again toss the glove in disgust. Indeed, he gets that third grounder. And he botches it yet again. And how does he react? He throws the glove <u>at</u> the runner on second who is now trotting past. This explodes our expectations, with this funny surprise.

Our example of the verbal "three" comes from *Ferris Bueller's Day Off*. Recall the moment when Ferris Bueller takes his friend, Cameron, to the private "showroom" garage that houses the fated Ferrari:

> CAMERON
> 1958 Ferrari 250 GTS California. Less than a hundred were made. My father spent years restoring it.

(This background sufficiently raises the stakes of the importance of what we see — and sets up that ticking clock of inevitability of destruction...)

> CAMERON
> It is his love...

(This is dialogue set-up #1)

> CAMERON
> It is his passion...

(This is dialogue set-up #2, establishing our pattern, and sending us in one direction of logic.)

> FERRIS
> It is his fault he didn't lock the garage.

(Ferris's surprise response derails the logical pattern established by Cameron's first two lines. This gives laughter. It also firmly establishes the ticking clock of inevitability that the Ferrari is fated for destruction.)

THE RUNNING GAG

What is it about "threes" that are funny? The three is clean. It's simple. We set up the logical pattern in two, and derail it with the third time. More than three can dilute the humor.

But a comic writer can use numerous repetitions throughout a story. These are generally referred to as **running gags**, a recurring event or character behavior (tic or flaw) that we come to expect each time the event occurs or the character appears. For example, Oliver Hardy twiddling his tie, and Stan Laurel scratching the top of his head. Or the inability of anyone in *Snatch* to understand a word coming from the mumbling mouth of Brad Pitt's character. Reversals of these running gags may eventually play out — giving laughter. Or they can be used repeatedly to entrench the character.

THE TOPPER

The **topper** is a final punctuation to a joke, the ultimate peak. In an exchange of dialogue, the topper is the last word, or final comeback.

In Neil Simon's *The Odd Couple*, when Oscar and Felix are at the crisis of their friendship:

```
          FELIX
I want to know if you're going to spend
the rest of your life not talking to me.
Because if you are, I'm going to
buy a radio.
```

                    OSCAR
You had your chance to talk
last night.
          (takes key out of pocket)
There's a key to the back door.
If you stick to the hallway
and your room, you won't get hurt.

                    FELIX
Meaning what?

                    OSCAR
Meaning that if you want to live here,
I don't want to see you, I don't want
to hear you and I don't want to smell
your cooking. Now get this spaghetti
off my poker table.

                    FELIX
Ha, ha, ha.

                    OSCAR
What the hell's so funny?

                    FELIX
It's not spaghetti, it's linguini.

Oscar picks up the plate of linguini, crosses to
the doorway of the kitchen and hurls it up and
into the kitchen.

                    OSCAR
Now it's garbage!

The topper can be an effective exclamation point to a physical gag as in
the unexpected topper in Keaton's *One Week*. Looking at the aftermath

of the train wreck, Buster puts a "For Sale" sign on the pile of kindling. The topper of the topper? Buster leaves the instructions for building the house and walks off with his bride.

The writer can also add a visual action to top a verbal exchange. Sometimes words aren't enough and we have to resort to the "last word." In *Tootsie*, Michael Dorsey tries to convince his agent to field his auditions. He can't believe his agent's insistence that Michael cannot get a job — and Michael ends the argument with a childlike defiant "Oh, yeah?" That's not the topper — the topper comes in the next scene. A visual topper with Michael Dorsey walking down a busy New York street dressed as Dorothy Michaels going off to his audition.

And, in fact, that is the topper of this exploration of the physical properties that make comedy work. Now let's explore some Tenets of Laughter.

THE 3
TENETS OF
LAUGHTER

Comic writers and comedians often claim there are no rules in writing comedy. And, in fact, comedy is by its very nature a form of revolt, a breaking of rules and laws, a surprise element that gives us our laughter response.

However, we present in this chapter universal guidelines or tenets that are present in every successful comedy. These new perspectives or layers assist our understanding of how comedy works. They result in our intended payoff: that of audience laughter.

To help illustrate these tenets, and give clear examples that you will understand, we've chosen five comedies to break down according to these tenets. We've selected comedies that should be familiar to you. Yet, they are distinctive and unique in order to show the universality of these tenets.

Feel free to hold these tenets up to any of your personal favorite comic bits and stories to better understand why they work.

THE FILMS:

Some Like It Hot (1959)   Screenplay by Billy Wilder and I.A.L. Diamond. Directed by Billy Wilder.

The Pitch: *Two out-of-luck cads witness the St. Valentine's Day massacre and disguise themselves as female musicians to flee from the mob.*

Ghostbusters (1984)   Written by Dan Aykroyd and Harold Ramis. Directed by Ivan Reitman.

The Pitch: *A trio of paranormal experts set up a ghost-busting business in New York City.*

Ferris Bueller's Day Off (1986) Written and directed by John Hughes.

The Pitch: *High-school trickster Ferris feigns sickness to take a day off to help give his best friend a needed shot of self-esteem.*

Shrek (2001) Written by Ted Elliott & Terry Rossio and Joe Stillman and Roger S.H. Schulman. Based on the book by William Steig. Directed by Andrew Adamson and Vicky Jenson.

The Pitch: *A reclusive ogre rescues a princess from a dragon in order to win back his swamp.*

Bridget Jones's Diary (2001) Screenplay by Helen Fielding and Andrew Davies and Richard Curtis. Based on the novel by Helen Fielding. Directed by Sharon Maguire.

The Pitch: *Fed up with her life, Bridget Jones vows to maintain her New Year's Resolution by keeping a diary of her hopeful transformation toward personal growth and love.*

TENET 1 – COMEDY IS CONFLICT AND COLLISION

A writer tackling a comedy script for the first time may believe that comedy is just a string of jokes. (Sadly, some Hollywood executives believe the same thing.) Yet, the foundation of comedy is **conflict**.

As we've discovered in the previous chapters, laughter comes from an unexpected collision of ideas or realities. The simplest, most powerful of one-lines from the great Henny Youngman, "Take my wife... please!" is steaming with conflict. Great comic teams: Laurel and Hardy, Abbott and Costello, Burns and Allen, Martin and Lewis, Bart and Homer give us the greatest laughter in bits, skits, and scenes when they are in conflict. The greatest comedy as selected by the American Film Institute, *Some Like It Hot*, has a premise based on the life-or-death conflict of a pair of musicians on the run from the mob. Conflict cannot be ignored in comedy. And the writer should be aware of conflict and its different levels to adequately develop a story and take advantage of its comic potential.

What is conflict? A character wants something very badly and comes up against forces of opposition. It could be two people after the same goal, and the dramatic question is who will win?

It isn't until someone else wants something that we start fighting for it (or at least realize how valuable that goal is). Taking it a step further, and forgive us for being morbid, but the central theme that makes Joseph Campbell's *Hero's Journey* so universal, and significant, is that it is based on death. By facing death, either literal or symbolic (the break-up of a relationship, firing from a job, eviction, banishment, etc.), one realizes what is worth fighting for. In romance, we say that distance makes the heart grow fonder. A lover goes away and that separation makes us realize how important that relationship is. If it's most important, we'll do everything we can to win it back. If we realize that it isn't that important, we'll go somewhere else depending on our priorities.

THE CENTRAL CONFLICT IS DEFINED BY A PROBLEM THAT MUST BE SOLVED

Every successful story is about a problem that must be solved. This defines and locks in the central conflict of the story.

You can define the problem as a goal that the character must attain. A goal means something that must be fought for, so it better be important. Or you can describe a goal as a problem that must be solved. "Solving" a problem implies difficulty and obstacle. Either way is fine, as long as you grasp the key here. Solving the central problem helps define the conflict of your story.

Here are the central problems as established within the first act of our sample films:

Some Like It Hot: To escape the mob.
Ferris Bueller's Day Off: To get a day off without getting caught.
Ghostbusters: To run a successful ghost-busting business.
Shrek: To get back the swamp.
Bridget Jones's Diary: To turn her life around.

THE CENTRAL PROBLEM CAN BE PHYSICAL (EXTERNAL), OR EMOTIONAL (INTERNAL)

The **physical goal** is something that requires physical action to achieve. And the goal itself is physical, it can be "held in the hand" so to speak. Shrek's reclaiming of his swamp is a physical goal. As is Joe's and Jerry's need to flee mob boss, Spats Columbo, in *Some Like it Hot*.

The **emotional goal** is something that serves our inner needs, and is achieved from within our bodies or psyches. Love, acceptance, strength, self-esteem, and redemption are all emotional or internal goals that can be achieved. Bridget Jones' desire to turn her life around is filled with emotional significance.

A successful story need not have a main character with both types of needs. Although you'll find that many of our more memorable stories have both types of problems that need to be solved.

YOUR COMIC STORY MAY BE SIMPLE OR COMPLEX

Although these central problems may be set up in the opening of the story, they may change depending upon the forces at work. This characterizes whether we are developing a simple or complex story.

In a **simple story**, the character's central problem is established in the beginning of the story, and the question is answered in the end. The same central problem is tracked throughout the story.

For example, in *Some Like It Hot*, although love complicates the journey, the central problem is sustained throughout the story: to escape the mob.

Bridget Jones seeks to resurrect her ideal life, with all of its complications, throughout. And that's tracked throughout the story, even though a deeper theme of being true to oneself is discovered during the course of her journey.

On the other hand, a **complex story** is one in which a central problem is initially established, but the course of the journey presents a deeper, more important question that takes focus.

In *Shrek*, the lovable ogre needs to win back his swamp and reclaim his solitary life. But in the course of the journey, he realizes that he really needs the Princess's love and share his swamp with her. Reclaiming his swamp is no longer the central question. Winning her love is. That is the true elixir we hope he celebrates in the end.

Ghostbusters also offers a complex story. The trio begins wanting to create a successful ghost-busting business. But the deeper problem is saving New York City from Gozer and its evil plan.

In both *Shrek* and *Ghostbusters*, the complex aspect is discovered by the character and the audience *at about the same time*. In *Ferris*

Bueller's Day Off, Ferris' real goal is to give best friend Cameron a shot of self-esteem. Ferris knows this, *but the audience doesn't*. So the story isn't simply about a boy playing hooky, but something much deeper, much richer.

THE CENTRAL PROBLEM LOCKS THE STORY'S CENTRAL ACTION AND ESTABLISHES THE CENTRAL DRAMATIC QUESTION

This central problem helps define the story's spine in several ways. It sets the **central dramatic question**, which is what the audience is asking while they are watching the film. They've invested time and money to find out the answer, and we hope that the question is significant enough to keep their butts glued to their seats.

The central dramatic question may change during the course of the story. So, for our sample films, by the end of the first act, the central dramatic question is that which the audience is probably asking:

Some Like It Hot: Will Joe and Jerry escape the mob?
Ferris Bueller's Day Off: Will he get a day off without getting caught?
Ghostbusters: Will the Ghostbusters succeed?
Shrek: Will Shrek get back his swamp?
Bridget Jones's Diary: Will Bridget turn her life around?

THE CENTRAL PROBLEM ALSO DEFINES THE SPECIAL WORLD OF THE STORY

Every story offers a **special world**, either physical or emotional. By committing to solving the problem, the character has entered this special world. Shrek physically must leave his swamp in order to win it back, and he's issued the task of rescuing the princess from the dragon. His commitment sends him into a special world of new lands and physical adventure. The Ghostbusters establish a business and commit themselves, heart, body, and mind to finding and exterminating ghosts. Again, a physical — okay, paranormal — world. But it

38

defines a special world that the character will commit to. In order to escape the mob, Joe and Jerry dress up as women and join an all-girls band. A very visual, physical special world.

In some tales, we enter an emotional special world. These stories often deal with character growth or healing as the central dramatic force. In comedy, we see these in romantic comedies and coming-of-age stories (i.e., *When Harry Met Sally*, *Fast Times at Ridgemont High*, *American Graffiti*, *Sixteen Candles*). Bridget Jones commits herself to her problem of self-development and love — an emotional special world.

But a character and a central goal isn't sufficient to lock the story's central conflict. Something has to get in the way of the hero solving the problem. This obstacle is what creates conflict. Although specifying the central problem suggests that it won't be an easy task, the story next needs to specify the forces of opposition. According to Elia Kazan, drama is two dogs fighting over a bone. The goal is the bone. One dog is your central character. Now you need the other dog or there isn't any drama — or comedy.

WITHOUT CONFLICT, THERE IS NO STORY — OR COMEDY

Why must we have conflict? Without conflict, there's no drama, no tension. We know that the hero will succeed, so frankly why should we-the-audience care? Also, as we'll discover in our next tenet, without conflict we never really test the conviction of our characters.

Let's look briefly at the first act of *Ghostbusters*. Our gang loses their funding, and their academic positions, before they find their niche by starting a ghost busting business.

But they have to prove themselves to the city (and to themselves). Their first encounter sends them running from the Public Library.

Their second encounter is a mixed success at the hotel ballroom. Yes, they captured their first ghost, they've also destroyed the ballroom in the process.

But there are nastier ghouls in the works and Gozer and the terror dogs are cooking up some master plan. We are hooked by this point. Will our hapless ghost busters succeed? And how?

CONFLICT REVEALS CHARACTER

Audiences love watching characters get themselves out of messes. With comedy, we usually expect unusual and surprising — often subversive and shocking — ways in which characters get out of a scrape. These help reveal true comic character.

Ferris Bueller, Bridget Jones, Shrek, each of the Ghostbusters (Venkman, Stantz, Spengler), Joe and Jerry are great characters that will address and overcome obstacles according to their background, beliefs, morals, and every other dimension that creates the comedic persona.

THE FOUR LEVELS OF CONFLICT

We can categorize conflict according to four groups or levels.

1. Inner Conflict: **Man versus himself**.

These conflicts are our inner doubts, inferiorities, fears, convictions, inflated egos, and emotional flaws that make decisions and actions difficult in our lives. An inner conflict can be an exaggerated comic flaw that becomes a major obstacle in the story — Michael Dorsey's chauvinism, Dumb and Dumber's stupidity, Inspector Clouseau's bumbling. A character's inner conflict can be the richest in your stories because it suggests character flaws that may be overcome and therefore offer the possibility of character development and growth. But the conflicts must be visual in some way. The audience needs to see this inner struggle, and externalizing a character's inner struggle can

40

give your story its most memorable moments. One of the funniest moments in *Liar Liar* is watching Jim Carrey (cursed by his son's birthday wish to tell the truth) trying to lie to his hand. A simple externalized inner struggle in *Ferris Bueller's Day Off* is Cameron's tantrum outside his car as he's trying to talk himself out of joining up with Ferris. The most painfully truthful moments in *Bridget Jones* are when she's alone, coping with her failures and deflated self: alone watching *Fatal Attraction*, dreaming she's being eaten by Alsatian dogs.

2. Interpersonal Conflict: **Man versus another person**.

This is the most common level of conflict explored in stories. A person wants something from someone else, or tries to convince someone to do something. All stories need interpersonal conflict.

3. Global Conflict: **Man versus his world**.

Global conflicts can additionally be broken down into man's conflict with society (the law, the military, the church, the school, etc.); man's conflict with situation (place or location); or man's conflict with the forces of nature (hurricanes, blizzards and other natural disasters). Societal conflicts are defined by a group or social structure that may be represented by an individual (police officer, teacher, MP). The situation or environment can be an important conflict in slapstick, where the comic hero is battling everyday items and constraints of location.

4. Cosmic Conflict: **Man versus the cosmos** (God, Devil, Fate, Time).

These cosmic forces may be acknowledged by a character, but not necessarily confronted directly. In *Sleepless in Seattle*, fate is a significant force determining Annie's search for love. Time is an important cosmic conflict in *Groundhog Day*. God is a strong force in *Monty Python and the Holy Grail*, as is the Devil in *The Witches of Eastwick*.

Let's look at some of the key levels of conflict from the sample films:

Some Like It Hot

Inner Conflict: Joe's self-gratification in his hot pursuit of women; disguised as Shell Oil Jr., Joe's inability to be turned on by a woman (a deception used to seduce Sugar); Joe versus his feminine disguise Josephine; Joe versus his second disguise, Shell Oil Jr.; Jerry versus his feminine disguise Daphne.
Interpersonal Conflict: Joe versus Jerry; Joe/Junior versus Sugar; Jerry/Daphne versus Osgood.
Global Conflict: Joe and Jerry versus the mob; Joe and Jerry versus the band; Joe and Jerry versus the confined train car.
Cosmic Conflict: No strong cosmic conflicts.

Ghostbusters

Inner Conflict: Peter Venkman's inflated ego; the Ghostbusters' lack of experience.
Interpersonal Conflict: The trio of Ghostbusters against themselves; Peter Venkman versus Dana; Dana versus the nebbish neighbor, Louis.
Global Conflict: The Ghostbusters versus the school; the Ghostbusters versus the city of New York; the Ghostbusters versus the E.T.A.; the Ghostbusters versus the ghosts.
Cosmic Conflict: The Ghostbusters versus Gozer; the Ghostbusters versus the Stay-Puft Marshmallow Man.

Ferris Bueller's Day Off

Inner Conflict: Cameron's lack of self-esteem, Ferris' confidence.
Interpersonal Conflict: Ferris versus his sister; Ferris versus Dean Rooney; Ferris versus his parents; Ferris versus Cameron.
Global Conflict: Ferris' sister versus the student body that is rallying behind Ferris; Ferris versus Chicago; Ferris versus the neighborhood when he's trying to race home before his parents arrive; Dean Rooney versus the Bueller house.

42

Cosmic Conflict: Fate. Ferris has several near misses of being discovered by his father, and Dean Rooney.

Shrek

Inner Conflict: Shrek's loneliness.
Interpersonal Conflict: Shrek versus Donkey; Shrek versus Princess Fiona; Donkey versus Dragon.
Global Conflict: Shrek versus the fairy tale creatures; Shrek versus Lord Farquaad's knights; Shrek and Donkey versus the Dragon's lair.
Cosmic Conflict: Princess Fiona's curse.

Bridget Jones's Diary

Inner Conflict: Bridget's loneliness and insecurity with self.
Interpersonal Conflict: Bridget versus Mark Darcy; Bridget versus Daniel Cleaver; Darcy versus Cleaver; Bridget versus her mum; Bridget's mum versus Bridget's dad.
Global Conflict: Bridget versus her family's friends; Bridget versus her fellow employees.
Cosmic Conflict: No strong cosmic conflicts.

Each level of conflict requires different levels of resources for overcoming the conflict. The way we deal with our inner conflicts reveals a different aspect of ourselves compared with overcoming obstacles presented by relationships, the environment, or God.

BUILDING YOUR LEVELS OF CONFLICT

Often you need to evaluate the levels of conflict, to fertilize the fields for comedy.

Let's say we're writing a revenge story about an ordinary Joe trying to get back at his abusive boss. Joe has always bowed to others, and the boss is greasing the company books. The executive suits are moving in on the boss, but he's sufficiently cooked the books with Joe as the main course of blame. This establishes three levels of conflict:

Inner: Joe's low self-esteem.
Interpersonal: Joe versus his boss.
Global: Joe versus the law, the corporate suits.

This has finally pushed Joe to overcome his inner conflict (low self-esteem) to get revenge. He discovers that his boss has the real books hidden away in his home safe. Okay, logically why wouldn't the boss destroy the books? He's an obsessive pack rat, and paranoid — he doesn't trust shredders.

So Joe plans this great break-in to steal the original books and screw the boss. A new level of conflict:

Global: the boss's house (security system, the safe, etc).

For an insecure comic hero who's never broken the law, we can imagine the comic moments here. (Yes, his lack of experience in breaking the law becomes an inner conflict.)

Can we make it more difficult for him?

Perhaps he has to break in when the boss is asleep upstairs? That could work. Perhaps, the boss is having an affair with Joe's wife, and has her in bed upstairs? That could be torturous, and painfully funny (painful for Joe, funny for us).

We could put in the oft-used guard dog. But let's say the boss hates dogs, and has a couple of cute, friendly kitties.

Now we have another potential obstacle — kitty-cats. How can we use this against Joe to make it even more difficult for him? He's allergic to animal hair. This new inner conflict materializes into a global/environmental conflict when he confronts the friendly kitties in the boss's office, while the boss and Joe's wife are having a great time in the other room.

We haven't addressed any cosmic levels of conflict. Has fate always given Joe the raw end of the deal? Has he turned away from God, but is now trying to resurrect his religion? Does Joe make a Faustian pact with the Devil to get the strength and will power to get revenge?

We're riffing here, and we may end up keeping some of this material or discarding it. The point is that acknowledging the different levels of conflict can open up the comic potential in your story. You may be generally limiting your levels of conflict in the stories you're currently writing. Look at some of your past stories and track the levels of conflict. You may discover that you tend to tap the same one or two levels of conflict (the most common are relational and global). Try exploring other levels to build the comedy.

You do not have to pile on the conflicts.

Too much conflict can muddy a story. You may not need all these levels of conflict. Many successful romantic comedies focus on interpersonal and inner conflicts.

THE COMIC POWER OF COLLISION

Laughter rises from the **collision** of two very different ideas, presenting a surprise punch line or incongruity.

One of the most popular structures of comedy is the fish-out-of-water tale. Simply defined, the central character (the "fish") is placed in a world completely out of his or her element, a collision of the ordinary and special worlds. Building the contrast between the fish's natural element and the world they enter can give the collision greater impact, and greater laughs. In *Shrek*, the central hero called to save the beautiful Princess Fiona from the dragon isn't the Jack of Beanstalk fame or Prince Charming, but a hideous, reclusive ogre named Shrek. So, *Shrek's* central conflict can be seen as the collision of a hideous, reclusive ogre and our image of a typical heroic rescuer.

Collision can happen from characters and goals.

COLLISION OF CHARACTERS

Character collision is an important aspect in any comedy. Building character contrast can expand your arena for comic collision. Contrast can come from personality traits, goals, motivations, and individual comic perspective (i.e., the character's unique take on the world).

The buddy comedies and comic teams require contrast for laughs. One member can be seen as the serious one, the "straight man," and the other as the fool. One sets up the joke, the other delivers the punch line. They need each other for the joke. For example, in Neil Simon's *The Odd Couple*, Felix and Oscar alone in their own worlds may not be very funny. But the collision of their worlds in one apartment explodes in comic situations. Simon fuels the fire of comedy by putting these characters at polar opposites. Oscar is the ultimate slob, and Felix the neat freak.

In romantic comedy, the collision and comic potential comes from the contrast of the two potential lovers. This can be established in their respective ordinary worlds. By sharing, enforcing, disguising, or sacrificing their respective worlds, they may discover a common bond that opens the heart for love. In *Shrek*, the initial collision of hideous ogre Shrek and beautiful Princess Fiona leads to comic conflict, until they begin to strip away the truth of a common bond. Princess Fiona lives a secret curse, causing her to live at night as an ogre.

In *Some Like It Hot*, Jerry is the worry-wart, always doubting success

46

and anticipating failure. Joe is the self-serving buddy, whose pursuit of self-gratification gets them deeper into trouble.

Ferris Bueller is the ultimate trickster. Everything has been pre-planned, every detail and reaction anticipated in his plot to foil the school establishment. His world collides with Dean Rooney, a polar opposite armed with an obsession for upholding the rules.

COLLISION OF GOALS, NEEDS, AND DESIRES

The collision can be defined by the contrast of goals, needs, and desires. Ferris wants the day off. Dean Rooney wants Bueller's ass glued to his desk chair. Shrek discovers that he's in love with Princess Fiona. Lord Farquaad needs to marry Fiona to become a legitimate king. In *Bridget Jones*, both Cleaver and Darcy want Bridget. And she, too, is torn between these two men. These are all examples of collision of goals.

A CHARACTER CAN SEEK AN INNER NEED THAT THREATENS THE OUTER GOAL

The collision can happen within the character, as internal/emotional goals can conflict with external/physical goals. Shrek initially wants to restore his solitary life, but his physical journey to deliver the princess to Lord Farquaad unlocks an inner need, his need to share his life with another, Princess Fiona. Joe and Jerry need to escape the mob and maintain their disguises as women; however, Joe's selfish need to seduce Sugar threatens their journey's success.

BUILDING CONFLICT AND COLLISION WITH EFFECTIVE SUBPLOTS

We've focused primarily on how the story's central conflict, character goals, and ordinary worlds can facilitate collision and comic payoff. Secondary conflicts and subplots can further complicate the comic

47

hero's journey and build comic potential. There are several ways to weave and structure secondary conflicts and subplots.

SNOWBALLING CONFLICTS

The consequences of overcoming one obstacle or conflict can raise the stakes, and jeopardize the hero's success. This snowballing can be a series of deceptions that gets your comic hero deeper and deeper into the world. *Some Like It Hot* shows the classic example of the gender-reversal disguise. Joe and Jerry commit to their special world as women in an all-girl band. That alone may be enough to sustain the central conflict, but they get deeper into the deception when Joe takes on a new disguise as Shell Oil Jr. in order to seduce Sugar Kane. Jerry/Daphne is enlisted to keep Osgood busy on shore, while Joe uses the yacht for the seduction. But the snowballing/complications continue when Osgood proposes to Jerry/Daphne, and he/she accepts! This simmers the farcical stew and the boiling point is reached when Spats Columbo arrives at the hotel.

As Ferris takes greater risks in his need to get the last, great day off from school, the potential for the revelation of his deception becomes more immediate. A snowballing is built by Ferris placing Cameron's dad's car in the hands of the parking attendant, going to the same restaurant as his father, attending the Cubs game, turning Chicago's German-American Day parade into a "Twist and Shout" free dance, escalating until Cameron's apparent breakdown, and climaxing with Ferris' mad chase to get home before his parents.

STRIPPING AWAY OF CONFLICTS

Some stories can show a stripping away, abandonment, or sacrifice of elements of the hero's life, until the most important thing in life is all that's left. We often see this in the classic screwball comedy (i.e., *Bringing Up Baby*), where the trickster socialite woman torments the working class hero, methodically destroying elements of his ordinary world (and those goals he was trying to achieve) until all he's left with is love.

In *Shrek*, the first act shows Shrek stripped of his ordinary world. He must leave his swamp, now populated by the fairy tale creatures, to win back his solitary life. Distanced from his swamp, he gradually realizes that he seeks something more, something he rebelled against in the ordinary world: companionship and love.

Bridget Jones goes through a similar stripping away of her ideal life as written in the diary — until she finds and fights for her true love, Mark Darcy, the one who learns to love Bridget for who she is.

EPISODIC CONFLICTS

Episodic conflicts are a sequence of conflicts that must be overcome by the hero for success of the overall goal. Although the "episodes" contribute to the overall success or failure of the journey, they may not compound upon each other.

In many "Road" comedies (Hope and Crosby's *Road to Bali* etc., *Flirting with Disaster*, *Pee-wee's Big Adventure*, *Maverick*) the overall destination is the primary goal. Obstacles are encountered on the road, but these may not build upon other conflicts. Essentially an episodic conflict is overcome and the character moves on. Doing so helps the overall journey, but the hero can move on without any consequences due to overcoming that particular conflict.

One could argue that some of Ferris' events that he enjoys are episodic in nature: the Cubs game, the parade. The Ghostbusters also overcome episodic conflicts (buying the abandoned firehouse) that move them along their journey, but do not necessarily complicate the central conflict.

EXERCISES:

1. What is the central problem that your character needs solved?

2. What are the levels of conflict?

3. Riff or brainstorm using all levels of conflict. What are all of the potential conflicts that could happen in your story? Remember, these conflicts are not set in stone. Explore the possibilities and then edit or discard according to what works best for the story you are trying to tell.

4. Look at some of your past stories (especially projects that haven't sold or you've abandoned) and evaluate the levels of conflict you tend to use in your storytelling. Can you mine other levels of conflict to give your story more comic potential, for urgency in the telling?

TENET 2 – COMEDY IS CONVICTION

One of the great moments in movie history is the scene in *The Gold Rush* in which Charlie Chaplin eats his own shoe. Snowbound in a mountain cabin, without hope, without food, Charlie is provided with sufficient stakes to sacrifice his footwear for Thanksgiving Dinner. Charlie eats his share of the well-cooked boot, twirling the laces like spaghetti, and picking the shoe's nails clean of any last morsel. This is a man savoring every bite of what could be his final meal. That simple image shows the power of **character conviction**.

It isn't enough that the character needs something or needs to solve a goal. It must be important. Something must be at stake if the goal isn't achieved.

50

And if the motivation is sufficient enough, the character will do almost anything to solve it. Charlie sacrifices his shoe in one comic moment. Joe and Jerry sacrifice their identities as men to escape the mob. Shrek leaves his crowded swamp in order to reclaim his solitary one. Embarrassment and a ticking clock of spinsterhood, push Bridget Jones to attempt to transform her life.

Motivation needs to be strong. It has to be important enough for the character. Even with many children's stories, the conviction must be important enough from the perspective of the characters. Their levels of need may not seem as significant from the grownup's perspective, but children have to be able to identify with their values.

CONVICTION HELPS REVEAL TRUE CHARACTER

True character is revealed by action when faced with the situation at hand. By raising the stakes, building the levels of conflict, and making it difficult for the character, we learn how far he or she will go.

Yes, call it a challenge if you will. To what lengths will the character go to get what they're after? Don't forget, if it isn't important enough for the character, why would it be important for the audience? Extending the character until they utilize their unique resources, their "special powers," is the objective. These "special powers" help define the character and contribute to the comic arena.

COLLISION WITH THE SPECIAL WORLD CAN SHATTER YOUR CHARACTER'S INITIAL CONVICTION

Young Frankenstein begins with Frederick Frankenstein proclaiming to his medical students that his grandfather's work was "doo-doo." Yet, when he's given the keys to his grandfather's lab, and everything that comes with it, we see a quick demise of his initial conviction.

51

Joe and Jerry's special world helps them get in touch with their feminine nature, giving them new power to find love and commitment with their respective partners.

Shrek's commitment to a solitary life is shattered during his journey. By journey's end, he is racing to stop the marriage and proclaim his love for the princess.

Bridget Jones learns to trust who she is and discard her initial ideal image.

TRUE CHARACTER IS BASED ON A CHARACTER'S SPECIAL POWERS

Ferris Bueller is a teen determined to play hooky. He's up against a formidable foe, Dean Rooney, who is just as determined to bust Ferris. What are the comic payoffs from this collision of these two characters' convictions?

Ferris shows his determination for success with his succession of deceptions to get his friends out of school. Although we are unaware of his motives, his determination as revealed by his actions tells us this has to be important for him. And most important, they reveal Ferris Bueller's essence of character.

Rooney is equally determined to bust Ferris. He tries to catch Bueller at home, but Ferris has rigged the home intercom with a recording. Rooney discovers this deception and attempts to break into the house, only to lose his shoe in the mud, and confront the family rottweiler. Overcoming these obstacles will not dissuade the principal from his goal.

This clash of convictions offers opportunity for comedy fueled by mistaken identities, misdirection, and slapstick embarrassment.

Ferris' conviction (motivation) is that this is the last opportunity to give his best friend some self-esteem. His special powers? He's incredibly, creatively resourceful, especially with the tools of teens: electronics, disguises, and quick action.

Dean Rooney can't let Ferris win and undermine the rules of the school and his authority. His conviction is revealed by his determination to bust Bueller — to the point of fault, as if he's wearing a pair of horse blinders on his eyes.

In contrast, Bridget Jones initially has her eyes set on Mr. Right, her boss, Daniel Cleaver (Hugh Grant). She uses all of her resources to catch his eye, get his attention, and finally match his seduction. She's won her goal only to have it blow up in her face when she discovers that he's been having an affair. This moment of truth and pain bursts Bridget's bubble and throws her into despair, but she is resurrected with a renewed strength to move on — a strength that later contributes to Cleaver's return and conviction to save their relationship.

In *Some Like It Hot*, two men flee from the mob. They also need money. So they get jobs as musicians in an all-girl band heading off to a gig at a Florida hotel. What would make their success most difficult, and test our two characters to the extent of their special powers? Put Marilyn Monroe as a member of the band, and make her all the more vulnerable when she reveals her weakness for sax players. Wouldn't you guess that Joe the cad plays the sax! Tempted by this eye-candy, Joe reveals his special powers of juggling multiple disguises, and turning the tables, to get Sugar Kane to seduce him! But this collision of external needs (escaping the mob) with internal needs (seducing Sugar) forces Joe to reveal his true self by the end of the picture, and he sacrifices all to escape with his life, his buddy, and his love.

THE AUDIENCE MUST RELATE TO THE CONVICTION ON SOME LEVEL

This aspect of comedy is all about getting the audience to invest themselves in the story. The audience needs to identify with the goals and motivations of all the characters — but especially those of the hero.

53

The motivation can serve a universal need (love, revenge, or righting a wrong). For the sports or crime comedy, it could be the underdog overcoming the opposition (slobs versus snobs, or the lowly grifter conning the crime boss).

If it is sufficient to fuel our empathy and identification, we'll be there pulling for the hero. If the goal is important enough for the character and that importance makes sense, then we'll be there, whether it's Shrek winning the princess, the Ghostbusters saving New York, or Pee-wee Herman finding his stolen bicycle.

DOES THE AUDIENCE HAVE TO KNOW THE MOTIVATION?

Frankly, writers can get too focused on building a character's motivation, creating the "skeleton in the closet." Often with comedy, KISS ("Keep It Simple, Stupid"). Sometimes the absurdity of the comedy comes because the character doesn't have much of a motivation at all.

Comedy is the trickster genre, and part of its nature is to break convention. Seek the absurd, and the exaggerated. So, is it possible to get comedy from a character with no real motivation? Why not? In *Monty Python and the Holy Grail*, King Arthur gets the call from God to find the Holy Grail. Why? Do his knights question it? They serve their king because that's what they do. Dr. Evil, Austin Powers' dominant opposition, plots evil plans because that is his evil nature.

THE STAKES MUST BE SUFFICIENTLY RAISED

Ask yourself: What can your characters afford to lose if they fail? Are the stakes sufficient to commit them to the journey ahead? They need to be. If not, then your characters could easily turn their tails if it gets too rough. Or your audience could quickly lose interest. The stakes can be effectively established in the story's ordinary world.

Joe and Jerry will lose their lives if they don't flee.
Shrek will lose his swamp.

54

The Ghostbusters lose their jobs and funding through the university. Bridget Jones refuses to become a spinster.

Initially, we are not aware of Ferris Bueller's motivation (and the stakes) for taking the day off. But we delight in watching this trickster youth outsmart the pillars of the parental and scholarly establishment.

EXERCISES:

> **1**. Test your character's conviction. Is the goal important enough? Are the stakes sufficiently raised? Will it be difficult?

> **2**. Is there sufficient conflict to reveal the true character of your lead?

> **3**. What are your character's special powers?

> **4**. How do the growing obstacles and raising of the stakes fuel conviction and reveal the comic character's special powers?

TENET 3 – COMEDY IS DECEPTION

As we learned in "The Physics of Funny" (Chapter Two), comedy often works on several levels of reality or meaning. The verbal joke has a set-up that establishes one reality, and the punch line delivers the unexpected collision of a second level or alternative meaning of the reality. This form of **deception** is necessary to produce our payoff: laughter. We are led to believe one reality, but we realize we've been deceived when the alternative meaning is revealed. Let's take apart Henny Youngman's classic one-liner: "Take my wife... please!" The deception is based on two meanings for the word "take." The set-up "Take my wife..." quickly establishes the first reality with "take" meaning "For example..." or "Consider..." Henny's going to tell us a story about his wife, right? Or so we are led to believe. The punch line "... please!" reveals his deception. "Take" actually means "Take her away."

55

This deception can work on a much larger scale in the comic story. A character is led to believe one level of reality, while another character, and the audience, is aware that this is all a deception. After their bumbling first capture of Slimer, the Ghostbusters start advertising as ghost-busting experts. The people of New York believe the advertisements and indeed they're having ghostly encounters so... "Who you gonna call?" Yet the audience is "in" on the deception. The Ghostbusters can hardly be considered experts in supernatural capture and disposal. Whether in a simple joke, or comic story line, suspense is held in anticipation of the punch line or revelation of this deception. The outcome: laughter.

Often the comic deception is very visual and obvious. Our comic hero believes he must be something different than he is in order to achieve the goal at hand. He takes on a disguise he feels best fits the objective.

The gender-bending comedies offer the most visual of deceptions. A man or woman dresses up as the opposite of what they are. So in *Mrs. Doubtfire*, we see Robin Williams disguised as a Scottish nanny in order to get closer to his kids. Steve Martin is possessed by Lily Tomlin in *All of Me*. The remake of *The Nutty Professor* is another visually strong deception. Extremely obese, self-conscious Sherman Klump, uses genetic experimentation to transform himself into his alter-ego, smooth-talking, svelte Buddy Love.

The deception doesn't have to be this visually extreme; however, in most successful comedies, we see some level of deception. A character creates a new guise for him or herself in order to successfully pursue the goal.

In *Back to the Future*, Marty McFly takes a DeLorean time machine and gets stuck in the 1950s. He can't tell people there that he's from the 1980s — that's his deception. When he runs into his teenage mother and father, he can't tell them he's their son, complicating the deception.

In *Deuce Bigalow: Male Gigolo*, the deception is that he's not a gigolo, but he has the opportunity to become one in order to fix the condo he's ruined.

In the caper comedies, the deception is often the con game created by our underdog team in their pursuit to con the mark.

In romantic comedy, lovers often feel self-conscious of their ordinary worlds. We protect who we really are because we're afraid of the pain of rejection. Lovers will create guises or deceptions to become the person we believe our partner would want.

In teen and coming-of-age comedies, the deception is that teens feel the need to act like adults in an adult world of love and work. Yet, they're still teens. And peer pressure to achieve the goals that are perceived as adult (i.e., losing one's virginity) often force characters to fabricate an over-inflated image of sexual prowess (a deception).

CAN YOU HAVE MORE THAN ONE LEVEL OF DECEPTION?

A story can have many layers of deception, as characters try to push for their individual goals. Farce as a form of comedy thrives on numerous deceptions, misunderstandings, and disguises.

In *There's Something About Mary*, Ben Stiller needs to find Mary, his true love from high school. He hires a private detective, a deception that Ben must try to keep from Mary. But the detective falls for Mary, and creates his own deception. He tries to get Ben Stiller off the case by creating an image of Mary as an overweight, divorcée invalid. The detective uses surveillance to help him "disguise" himself as the perfect man for Mary. In fact, there is something so special about Mary: We discover that all of the men have been using deception to pursue her.

THE STAKES MUST BE SUFFICIENTLY RAISED IN ORDER TO SEEK THIS PLAN OF DECEPTION

Earlier we discussed the need for sufficient stakes in order to commit to pursuing the character goal or objective — a good guideline for any story regardless of genre. But many successful comic premises are based on outlandish deceptions. The stakes must be sufficient to push this deception. If the stakes of success or failure are sufficiently raised, the comic hero should have nowhere else to go but pursue the deception.

Why seek the deception? We often don't trust that being truthful will give us what we desire. So, our comic characters may stumble upon at times outlandish deceptions to help them get what they want. Falling into the deception must make sense for our characters. The motivation and stakes must be raised sufficiently to accept this outlandish premise.

THE GREATEST COMIC PAYOFF: THE REVELATION OF THE DECEPTION

The more deceptions you place in your story, the more chances that the deceptions will be revealed. And the more people who become aware of the deception, the greater the chance of masks falling. This builds suspense in your comedy story, because the audience is anticipating that moment of revelation when the house of cards will fall. Often we cut to the comic chase as the hero desperately tries to maintain the deception as long as possible, or flee discovery, or race to claim what is most important.

One of the most satisfying moments in comedy is the revelation. The deception crumbles, and the character must fess up. One such moment of comic revelation is Michael Dorsey's in *Tootsie*. Stakes have been sufficiently raised to force him to drop the disguise of Dorothy Michaels during a live broadcast of the daytime drama.

The deceptions of our sample films:

Some Like It Hot

The guys have to dress up as girls to escape Spats Columbo and his thugs. Then Tony Curtis decides to disguise himself as Shell Oil Jr., a deception upon a deception that gets the two musicians deeper into trouble.

Ghostbusters

Professional ghost-busting is untried territory for them. They haven't even seen a ghost until they are called to the library. And although bumbling, they are trusted by New York as authorities. Supernatural villain Gozer is also working a grand deception (including the manipulation of Dana and Louis) that is progressively revealed and thwarted by the end of the journey.

Ferris Bueller's Day Off

The entire story is based on the ultimate teen fantasy deception — pretending to be sick to take the day off from school. This escalates until first school and then community (newspaper, police) are rallying behind the boy's health. This overall deception is built upon smaller deceptions that Ferris uses to get his way — getting his girlfriend out of school, getting a table for lunch. And Ferris' deeper deception is that he's using this day-off to help build his best friend's self-esteem. Ferris' two primary nemeses in his journey, sister Jeanie and Dean Rooney, believe the deception is just that, and are determined to bust him.

Bridget Jones's Diary

Her diary is the deception. This is what she is keeping from everyone. And she is forcing herself to be someone she isn't. She discovers, to her fear, that Cleaver has also worn a mask concealing his true self. Neither

59

Darcy nor Bridget sees each other for who they really are. Once this first impression is dropped, they begin to realize their love for each other, a love based on seeing each other for who they really are. Yet another deception is the lie that Cleaver has been spreading about how Darcy destroyed Cleaver's wedding.

Shrek

Shrek is the ultimate non-hero: a hideous ogre. He is kept masked until Princess Fiona demands to see her savior. She, too, is keeping back her deception, that she's cursed to spend her evenings as an ogre. Love's true kiss will turn all of this around.

EXERCISES:

    1. What is your hero's goal?

    2. How can deception be used to achieve the goal?

    3. Are stakes sufficiently raised to support pursuing the deception?

    4. Is there a moment when your character willingly needs to sacrifice the deception?

    5. Is there a moment when your character is forced to sacrifice the deception?

TENET 4 – COMEDY IS WISH-FULFILLMENT AND WORST FEAR

Comedy serves an audience's need for **wish-fulfillment**. It offers journeys of a trickster breaking rules, usurping the establishment, spouting witty comebacks, and often pursuing a reckless course of personal gratification. It can serve more gratifying needs of finding

60

our true love, or being the underdog and knocking our authority figures down in size.

It can be enjoyed vicariously through the ultimate heroic sacrifice. Stoic Buster Keaton overcoming fear, fate, and everything that our mechanized world can throw in his path to save his train and the girl in *The General*. Adam Sandler's water boy becoming a collegiate football star. These underdogs get the ultimate revenge whether it's a group of con artists led by Paul Newman and Robert Redford, or Dolly Parton, Jane Fonda, and Lily Tomlin in *Nine-to-Five*.

The concept of wish-fulfillment can help you structure your comic tale. If the audience is seeking comedy for satisfaction of this level of wish-fulfillment, then your characters can be seeking their specific wish-fulfillment scenario in the story. But isn't this as simple as the character having a goal? Yes, but what specifically is that goal? Is the achievement of the goal the fulfillment of your character's greatest wish? It could be.

Children's stories continually dish out tales that tap into the audience's greatest wishes. *Home Alone* gave us every kid's dream at some point in their lives — to have the house all to oneself! The only rules are no rules. In *Jimmy Neutron*, the parents have left town (wish-fulfillment: "Let's party all night"), but they've been abducted by aliens (worst fear: "Yikes, we're going to have to save them!")

PURSUIT OF THE GREATEST WISH CAN STRUCTURE THE ENTIRE STORY

The Ghostbusters want success, and all that comes with it (money, fame, stardom, women). As long as the ghosts are of a small nature, success seems to be assured.

Ferris Bueller gets the ultimate — and probably last — sick day of his illustrious high school career. He wants to make it the best.

A DEEPER WISH MAY DERAIL THE CHARACTER'S ORIGINAL WISH

Shrek's greatest wish is to get back his swamp and reclaim his solitary life. What he doesn't realize is that his inner wish is true love, which he could only discover after he goes off to retrieve Princess Fiona for Lord Farquaad.

Initially, Bridget Jones wants to transform herself from an overweight, smoking, and alcoholic woman into an "ideal" woman. She also has a relationship with her boss, Daniel Cleaver (a wish-fulfillment). But after he reveals his deceptive affair, Bridget begins to pull her life together and discovers that she really wants a lover who loves her for who she is.

The deeper wish that is discovered by Ferris Bueller is his goal of giving his friend, Cameron, a shot of self-esteem.

THE PURSUIT OF WISH-FULFILLMENT CAN THREATEN THE OVERALL GOAL

In *Some Like It Hot*, Joe and Jerry do not initially follow their greatest wish. Initially, they're just trying to get any paying gig to help them pay the bills and survive. Witnessing the St. Valentine's Day massacre sends them running into their special world dressed as women. But they step aboard an unbelievable wish-fulfillment: a sleeper train car filled with beautiful female musicians. Pursuit of this wish-fulfillment will jeopardize their deception.

Jerry (Jack Lemmon) is able to control his masculine urges, despite being placed in the position of fulfilling his ultimate wish: Marilyn Monroe offering herself in the middle of the night, wearing the skimpiest of nighties! Joe (Tony Curtis) on the other hand is determined to use deception to fulfill his greatest wish — seducing Monroe.

Remember the first tenet, "Comedy is Conflict and Collision?" So, to build the comic potential of your story, the pursuit of a character's greatest wish can be offset by the threat of the character's greatest fear.

COMEDY COMES FROM OUR GREATEST FEAR

The audience wants to see our greatest wishes fulfilled on screen, but we also delight in seeing the threat of failure. We laugh at comic reversals where the wish-fulfillment is quickly abandoned in the face our **greatest fear**. We laugh because it's not happening to us.

In the pursuit of our greatest wish, we want to see the worst thing that can happen. And when comedy works, the hero must face his worst fear. It could simply be the destruction of their plan, and the fear of embarrassment that they've been discovered. But in other journeys the worst fear may not be known until we suddenly discover ourselves facing it!

THE WORST FEAR CAN BE THE PRIMARY FORCE OF OPPOSITION

In *Home Alone*, Kevin gets the house, but taking care of the house all by himself until his parents return from Paris isn't enough to sustain a story. What would be his greatest fear? He has to defend the house against a pair of bumbling, yet determined, burglars. This collision of wish-fulfillment and greatest fear opens our world for comedy. It presents inevitability of events that must happen. How would an eight-year old defend his house against burglars?

Ferris Bueller's greatest fear is discovery by Dean Rooney. As Ferris pursues the greatest day off — getting away with a featured appearance at the German-American Parade, a brief television appearance during a Cubs game — the threat of the worst case scenario looms larger, and yet he's able to overcome every obstacle.

AWARENESS OF THE WORST FEAR CAN MAKE OUR HERO MOST RESOURCEFUL

Joe disguises himself as Shell Oil Jr. to seduce Sugar Kane. But he realizes that he can't take advantage of her. So he implements a masterful deception, feigning impotence to trick Sugar Kane into seducing him.

Putting our characters in a position where the pursuit of their greatest wishes collides with their worst fears offers some of our most memorable comic moments.

The Worst Fears in our Sample Films:

Some Like It Hot. Their greatest fear is that their disguises will fail. Remember when we left Jerry (as Daphne) in bed with Marilyn Monroe? The wish-fulfillment of revealing the disguise to have Marilyn collides immediately with the worst fear of having the disguise revealed. Later, Joe has a false sense of security when he pursues his wish-fulfillment, and soon after sweeping Marilyn off her feet, his worst fear (Spats Columbo) walks into the hotel.

Ghostbusters. Fear of failure is the Ghostbusters' greatest fear. And the appearances of Gozer, the terror dogs, and the Stay Puft Marshmallow Man are beyond their worst fears.

Ferris Bueller's Day Off. Cameron's worst fear that his father's car will be damaged is fulfilled. Ferris' worst fear is that his grand deception will be revealed, and that his parents or Dean Rooney will catch him.

Bridget Jones' Diary. One of Bridget's greatest fears is the revelation of her diary to either of her potential lovers. This fear becomes a reality in the final moments of the film.

Shrek. Shrek's worst fear initially is the loss of his swamp and solitary life. But by journey's end his greatest fear is losing Princess Fiona.

64

EXERCISES:

1. What is your character's greatest wish? Does this greatest wish define your character's central goal?

2. Is your character initially aware of this greatest wish? Or does your character discover it during the course of the journey?

3. What is your character's worst fear? Is the risk of facing this fear evident in your character's overall goal? (For example, Ferris Bueller wants to borrow Cameron's dad's prized 1961 Ferrari 250 GT California, but Cameron's worst fear is the discovery that he borrowed the car.)

4. How can this greatest fear collide with the character's greatest desire?

TENET 5 – COMEDY IS TRUTH

Comedy is for the common person, allowing us to laugh at ourselves and our situation. It's rooted in **truth**, the world we live in. Touching on subjects and story arenas that draw on common or shared aware ness can fuel audience identification. We know this story's world, and therefore we can better "get" the jokes.

Some common arenas that have been mined for successful comedy:

- Relationships, love, and sex
- Weddings
- Having a baby
- Being a single parent and having a baby
- Buying, remodeling a house
- Vacations
- Christmas
- School and college life

But truth in comedy also comes from the smaller moments, the honest, often painful reactions and situations that release a chuckle and tug our empathy. Bridget Jones arriving at a costume party dressed in a bunny outfit — not knowing that the costumes were called off. Later, after discovering that Cleaver has been having an affair, she walks alone on the street at night, devastated and still wearing the bunny outfit.

For the fantastic comic stories (*Ghostbusters*, *Big*), establishing the truth of your comic world is essential. Your audience needs to know the rules or reality of your world soon into the first act. The opening moments can be the most important in setting up your comic world. The paranormal powers are quickly established in the first moments of *Ghostbusters* when a librarian encounters a terrifying spirit. In *Big*, the magic world of the carnival sets up not only Josh's yearning to be "big," but the means to get his wish — the mechanical gypsy fortune-teller.

TENET 6 – COMEDY IS CHAOS AND ANARCHY

Comedy's prime target is authority and social mores. It's the trickster's role to disrupt the status quo in order to reveal society's problems. The ultimate revolt against social mores and authority is **chaos and anarchy**. In extreme anarchic comedy, structure falters, leaving the audience in chaos. In the final moments of *Monty Python and the Holy Grail*, police raid the production, haul off King Arthur as a suspect for murder, and finally force the cameraman to turn off the camera — and the movie. In a similar lampooning of the Hollywood Ending, Mel Brooks ends *Blazing Saddles* with a classic western chase and fight that breaks into a neighboring sound stage, interrupting the filming of a musical.

The Marx Brothers were the classic anarchistic tricksters. They sought any physical and verbal means to create havoc. Armed with physical roustabout, Harpo's silence, Chico's word reversals and puns, and Groucho's insults, the trio dished out their flamboyant, no-holds-barred disruption of social order and authority.

In contrast to the Marx Brothers' fueling chaos, W.C. Fields made his own personal mark portraying an anarchistic character barely hanging onto a life on the edge of chaos. His characters' lives were pulled in numerous conflicting directions due to the demands of authority figures, including a henpecking wife breathing down his neck. Fields bowed to these authority figures with his passive-aggressive brand of anarchy: under-his-breath insults, nonsensicals ("Godfrey Daniels!"), and a flask of bourbon. Oftentimes he was the butt of the joke. Yet on occasion, Fields did stand up to the one recurring character that could match him in anarchistic behavior — the obnoxious child.

The influence of these classic, anarchistic tricksters — tricksters contributing to breaking down all walls to society — can be seen in many memorable characters and movies. Bill Murray's John Winger disrupts the military in *Stripes*. The Delta House gang wreaks havoc at the homecoming parade in *National Lampoon's Animal House*. The comic voice of the Zuckers (*Airplane!*) and the Farrelly Brothers (*Dumb and Dumber*) rely on worlds and situations on the brink of complete devastation.

The environment itself can be out of control. This is an important characteristic of slapstick, where props, clothing, machines (anything from small appliances to cars), and homes can have a mind of their own, and seem out of control.

In the face of this anarchy and chaos, we lose control of socially accepted behavior and turn to our most childish and devilish instincts — the pie in the face, food fights, and tantrums. Often tormented characters shut down their facility to speak, resorting to gibberish, blubbering, and screaming. Out of necessity to overcome authority, a hero may seek these childlike behaviors to get their way. For example, Ferris uses childlike banter to sweet talk his parents and convince them he's sick.

Lack of control can lead to other embarrassing bodily releases including farts, belches, and pissing in one's pants. It's funny because it's trespassing on that which is deemed socially acceptable. And it taps back into our childish natures. No more pooping in your diapers, you have to learn to use the potty! Well, look over there, there's a doggy pooping on the lawn, and there's an elephant pooping in the center ring of the circus. And it's funny because the child has been told it's unacceptable.

Anarchy can also be seen as a comic hero's attempt to tackle too much. Whether serving self-gratification, or out of necessity, a comic hero juggles too many conflicting goals and deceptions. This frantic juggling ultimately leads to balls being dropped, forcing the comic hero to scramble or consciously decide what is worth fighting for.

In the midst of this juggling, the comic hero may need a character (some voice of reflection, conscience, or logic) to remind him or her that perhaps things are getting out of control. That character can warn the comic hero that he's gone too far. Or perhaps he can serve as a confidence booster to keep the comic hero focused on what's most important. The comic hero may be ready to hear it, then again, maybe not.

Jerry serves this role of the conscience voice in *Some Like It Hot*. And Joe refuses to hear it. Although Jerry has warned Joe not to pursue Sugar, it's the arrival of Spats Columbo that forces Joe to end the relationship.

In *Ferris Bueller's Day Off*, Cameron is this voice of reason. He tries to caution Ferris Bueller, always failing to turn Ferris around. But Cameron doesn't realize that Ferris is determined to see this day through because of its benefit to Cameron. It backfires when Cameron discovers the unaccounted mileage on his father's car and "freaks." But in an interesting twist, we soon realize that Cameron was faking this stone-faced seizure to fool Ferris.

In *Shrek*, Donkey becomes a key mentor figure to help Shrek and Princess Fiona focus and redirect their respective journeys.

Anarchy in the sample films:

In *Some Like It Hot*, every key moment and decision puts these characters on the fine line between balance and chaos. Stakes escalate in a madcap chaotic chase to resurrect their lives, their friendship, and their loves.

The Ghostbusters find themselves trying their damnedest to keep the supernatural plot at bay, but the EPA, and Gozer, turn New York City into chaos.

Ferris Bueller has complete control of his world. Everything is calculated. Every reaction from his foils is anticipated. Yet, he never anticipated that his lesson to his best friend would send Cameron over the deep end. Anarchy is also revealed in the destruction of Dean Rooney's world. This pompous figure of authority is gradually placed in a world out of his control — and manipulated by Ferris Bueller's ultimate plan.

Bridget Jones juggles two men, in addition to her commitment to transform herself (drop weight, stop smoking, etc). Just as she dumps one man, she realizes her love for the other. The center doesn't hold when Cleaver shows up unexpectedly at her birthday dinner. This leads to a fistfight between Cleaver and Darcy.

Shrek finds his solitary swamp thrown into crowded chaos when Lord Farquaad banishes the Fairy Tale Creatures. Shrek's journey is one to restore balance. But at every junction of his journey, things are on the verge of chaos.

EXERCISES:

1. What forces in your story are trying to promote chaos and anarchy?

2. What is your hero trying to juggle in your story? Are their conflicting goals that can lead to chaos and uncertainty?

3. How does your hero deal with the growing complications that are forcing chaos?

4. Does your hero need to make a sacrifice to restore balance?

4
COMEDY
AND CHILDREN

Children love to laugh. They offer a great, commercially-viable market for movies. But all too often writers of children's comedy run into two problems. First, they feel they need to "write down" (aka "dumb down") to some level that they believe kids will understand and appreciate. These writers end up using a limited spectrum of jokes, or relying upon the tried-and-true clichés that can quickly bore or exhaust the young mind. Truth is there are many more things children will laugh at than dog-doo jokes and ogre farts. The other quagmire writers can easily enter is the commercial obligation to include adults in the mix. But the writer focuses too much on attracting the adults, and ends up losing the tykes altogether. This chapter provides ways for the comic writer to broaden their perspective when writing for a children's audience.

LOOK AT THE WORLD THROUGH A CHILD'S EYES

Being a child is the comic perspective of children's tales. And yes, with their limited life experience, they often see stories on a different level than adults. For example, here are some of the major themes that children identify with:

- Acceptance with peers, friends and family
- Feeling different or an outcast
- Seeking independence
- Greediness and inability to share
- Standing up to bullies or grownups
- Importance of valued possessions
- Power of family and community

71

Writing for children requires seeing life from their perspective. It can be a fun journey back into your childhood, reclaiming your old memories and cherished toys. And much can be learned from seeing and exploring the world through children's eyes.

THE CHILDREN'S HERO

A child wants to be able to use his own unique special talents to defeat, confound, and trick all the forces of authority and conformity. The child constantly strives for independence in his own world, and a hero who can use the ordinary tools of the child in unique ways is easily embraced by the child audience. It gives them that strong "I'm like you" connection, and grants empowerment.

In *Home Alone*, Kevin invents ingenious ways to use a phonograph, model train, life-sized celebrities, strings, and pulleys to make the bandits believe that his home is inhabited. Later he booby-traps the house with common items to stop the robbery.

Ferris Bueller uses electronic equipment including tape recordings, timers, intercoms, telephones, and disguises to foil Dean Rooney.

Harriet the Spy, Nancy Drew, and the Hardy Boys use logic and ingenuity to crack the case.

The hero may indeed have unique special powers that are tapped or discovered:

Jimmy Neutron is a boy genius.

Harry Potter discovers his power of wizardry.

Matilda has the power to fulfill her deepest wishes.

The child audience member can identify with this, because each of us wishes we could have this type of special power. In the grown-up films we see this same audience identification in the majority of action adventure heros from Robin Hood to James Bond to Luke Skywalker.

The comic hero may be the trickster who usurps authority and tries to get away with it. All parents can identify with that important development stage for children during which they need to test the limits of authority. And those non-parents may be young enough to recall the stage. Just as comedy serves an important wish-fulfillment of seeking actions that are taboo in society, a child needs to see this as well.

Or the hero can be seen as flawed, unusual, and awkward. And children of all ages can easily identify with that.

CHILDREN RELISH A GOOD VILLAIN

Children eagerly latch themselves onto a character with whom they can identify, whether through personality or actions. They equally delight in seeing the nasty villain deservedly getting his comeuppance in the end. For this villain has the potential to represent the child's shadow or suppressed wants and desires (greed, selfishness, and need to hurt others). The villain's death can be a valuable moral lesson working on the child's psyche. Classic Disney animated films consistently served a deliciously evil shadow: Cruella De Ville in *101 Dalmations*, Ursala in *The Little Mermaid*, the Evil Queen in *Snow White*, Scar in *The Lion King*, Jafar in *Aladdin*.

These villains rarely have a comic aspect to them. Comedy comes out through a sidekick villain or perhaps through other subplots in the overall movie's structure. The villain is a very serious character.

But we could also turn someone or something children fear into a comic character like Captain Hook in *Peter Pan* — a buffoon, which helps children cope with their fear. Make fun of it, turn its evil into comic light (Sulley and the other monsters in the closet in *Monsters, Inc.*).

73

Shrek isn't just an ugly ogre but an endearing hero who can make a candle out of his ear wax and fart in his bath water.

All children's villains do not have to be composed of bona fide villainy. Just as satisfying is a villain who represents society or authority and needs a bit of cutting down to the child's size.

DEVELOPMENT OF CHILDREN'S HUMOR

The first level of humor that children seem to understand is purely physical and visual. Slapstick is extremely popular, especially when it builds on anticipation and release, reversals, exaggeration, the misuse of objects, and incongruous behavior.

As verbal skills expand, children can begin to relish wordplay, including puns and knock-knock jokes. Their understanding of the joke depends upon their life experience. As they get and retell these verbal jokes, they're building their self-esteem. In a verbal response to slapstick and visual incongruity, children also enjoy silly words and sounds. In their early school years, practical jokes are king, especially if the target is a well-deserved schoolyard bully. Yep, the poop jokes and other bodily functions are popular. Believe it or not, these jokes can help those 2-4 year olds alleviate some of that anxiety that was built up with potty training. But bodily function jokes are funny because they are taboo.

CHILDREN WILL LOOK FOR MEANING

As Aristotle suggests, every great art can teach and delight. The power to delight is fairly evident in cinema, but we often forget that story-telling of any kind also teaches. As audience members, it's difficult for us not to seek meaning from the stories we experience.

Kids can be in an extremely vulnerable position because they simply haven't had the life lessons of adults to judge how to take in and assimilate the actions they are experiencing in stories, whether it's a song, Saturday morning cartoon, or feature film.

Kids can't help it. All of us subconsciously seek meaning in the stories we experience. Kids aren't running to the theaters for morals and values, but this level of gathering meaning, mythic resonance, or life stories, works on a subconscious level. This is one reason why a child at a certain age will want to see a video, DVD, sing a song, and want to hear the same bedtime story or fairy tale over and over. They've latched onto some subconscious theme or story arc that feels pretty significant in their lives at that point of time.

COMIC 5
STORIES AND
THEIR STRUCTURE

Form is important. It allows the creative mind to focus one's story ideas. There isn't one generalized comic story, so we've broken this chapter into common comic stories, and used examples from several successful comedies to illustrate each structure. By understanding the mechanics of these specific forms, the comedy writer can effectively build his individual story. These are not "paint-by-numbers" story-telling patterns, but common recurring patterns and dynamics that we've distilled from these different forms. An important perspective of these story forms is the audience's. What are the audience's expectations when they see a romantic comedy or sports comedy? Understanding the payoffs of the story, and the expectations of the audience, while valuing your comic perspective and unique story-telling voice, grants surprises that will elevate your stories above the predictable comedies that often saturate the marketplace.

Our paradigm for examining these common structures is Joseph Campbell's *Hero's Journey*. This monomyth is well-recognized as a struc-tural paradigm in Hollywood. For readers unfamiliar with this powerful paradigm, a twelve-stage breakdown is included in this book's appendix. In *Myth and the Movies*, Stuart Voytilla shows how this paradigm allows us to better understand the characteristics of popular cinema genres. That resource is recommended for further reference.

In this section, we've gone deeper into the structure of comic stories and analyze ten common sub-genres:

- fish-out-of-water comedy
- romantic comedy
- sports comedy
- crime/caper comedy
- military comedy
- teen/coming-of-age comedy
- ensemble comedy
- farce
- black comedy
- satire, parody, and mockumentary

To warm you up for these chapters, let's take a few moments to define the important dynamics of the journey.

Every story is about a problem that must be solved by the characters of the story's world. This problem disrupts the initial balance or **ordinary world** of the story. Characters commit to solving the problem in order to restore balance.

The story's central problem defines the central dramatic question and importantly for these sub-genre discussions, the **special world** of the story that must be accepted.

We often see the three-act structure of story as a linear paradigm. A beginning (Act I), followed by a middle (Act II), followed by the end (Act III).

Story's Linear Structure

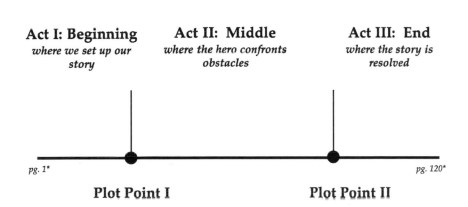

Act I: Beginning
where we set up our story

Act II: Middle
where the hero confronts obstacles

Act III: End
where the story is resolved

pg. 1*   pg. 120*

Plot Point I   **Plot Point II**

Plot Point: an event that spins the story into the next act.

*Page numbers indicate a two hour feature screenplay, where one page of script equals one minute of screen time.

79

A valuable model; however, *The Hero's Journey* goes deeper into the dynamics of three-act structure. First, fundamentally, describing story as a cycle:

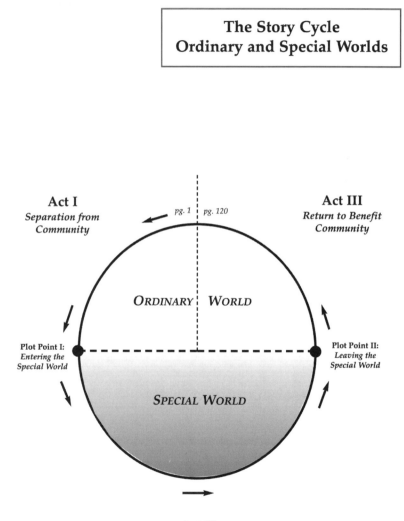

The Story Cycle
Ordinary and Special Worlds

Act I
Separation from
Community

pg. 1 | pg. 120

Act III
Return to Benefit
Community

ORDINARY | WORLD

Plot Point I:
Entering the
Special World

Plot Point II:
Leaving the
Special World

SPECIAL WORLD

Act II
Initiation into
the Special World

This cycle is seen initially as two halves, defined as the ordinary world and the special world, and represents a "rites of passage": separation from the community (Act I), initiation into the special world (Act II), and return with an elixir to benefit the community (Act III). The story's problem disrupts the ordinary world. The physical and/or psychological/emotional special world must be entered to tackle the problem. The problem must be significant enough and some level of death must be overcome in its pursuit. Physical or symbolic death and resurrection is a recurring pattern in any successful commercial story regardless of genre. By facing death, we learn what is worth fighting for. Therefore we see the acceptance of tackling the story's problem as a character's symbolic descent into the special world, as if the hero is physically descending into the underworld, tasting death to discover what is most important in life.

We can further divide this story cycle into four quadrants that describe the general pattern of addressing a problem. As seen in the following illustration, the linear three-act structure can be layered atop the quadrants, essentially creating four acts.

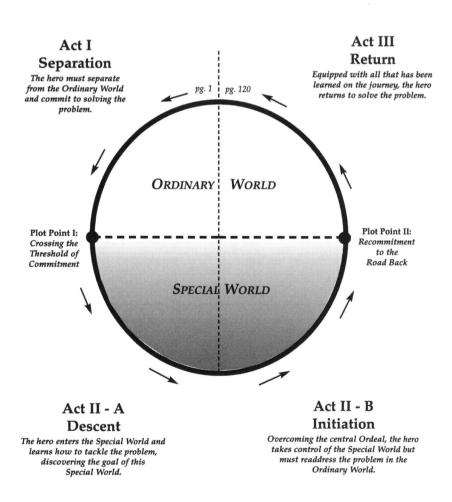

The Hero's Journey
as Story Quadrants

Act I
Separation
*The hero must separate
from the Ordinary World
and commit to solving the
problem.*

pg. 1 | *pg. 120*

Act III
Return
*Equipped with all that has been
learned on the journey, the hero
returns to solve the problem.*

ORDINARY | WORLD

Plot Point I:
*Crossing the
Threshold of
Commitment*

Plot Point II:
*Recommitment
to the
Road Back*

SPECIAL WORLD

Act II - A
Descent
*The hero enters the Special World and
learns how to tackle the problem,
discovering the goal of this
Special World.*

Act II - B
Initiation
*Overcoming the central Ordeal, the hero
takes control of the Special World but
must readdress the problem in the
Ordinary World.*

The quadrants and their general dynamics follow. (NOTE: The hero is the story's primary character or protagonist. The hero can be male or female, bug, or toy. In ensemble, team, or romantic comedies there can be more than one hero.) To keep this model rooted in comedy, we've included the popular and "you-better-know-this-classic" *Tootsie* as an illustration.

SEPARATION (ACT I)

The hero becomes aware of the problem that must be tackled. A **mentor** may be needed to alleviate any fears of taking the journey. When the stakes have been sufficiently raised, the hero crosses the threshold of commitment. In comedy, we often see the stakes raised to force the outlandish deception. In *Tootsie*, the stakes in this phase are sufficiently raised to force out-of-work actor, Michael Dorsey, to become budding actress, "Dorothy Michaels."

DESCENT (ACT IIA)

Upon entrance into the special world, the hero now must learn how to tackle the problem, and discover the central goal of this new world. Through tests, discovering allies and enemies, the hero tries to take control of this special world. Final preparations are made, as again stakes are raised forcing the hero to address a central ordeal that would determine the hero's victory of the special world. In comedy, this descent phase sees the hero taking command of his outlandish deception, but becomes tempted by the pursuit of a wish-fulfillment goal that complicates his problem, threatening the revelation of the deception. In *Tootsie*, Michael must take control of his special world in his new guise as Dorothy Michaels. He successfully gets the job on the daytime drama, and becomes a hit as a stronger woman role model. But his world is complicated when he falls for co-star Julie, his self-serving wish-fulfillment. As Dorothy, Michael becomes Julie's confidante and good friend. But as Michael, he fails at any potential relationship.

INITIATION (ACT IIB)

The hero survives the ordeal. He has proved victorious in the special world and earns or steals the reward he was after. But now the stakes are sufficiently raised to push, chase, or coax a recommitment to return to the ordinary world and solve the central problem. By the end of this quadrant, the hero is forced through the threshold bordering the special and ordinary worlds, a second plot point or **road back**. The pursuit of the outlandish deception collides with the comic hero's self-satisfying wish-fulfillment goal, and soon the hero finds himself juggling too much. The center cannot hold and the hero must decide what is most important. In *Tootsie*, Dorothy Michaels has become a major soap star. Michael has successfully earned the money he needs to produce his roommate's play. But as Dorothy, Michael becomes the target of several romantic advances from male friends, including Julie's father. And as Dorothy, Michael cannot win Julie's heart. The stakes are sufficiently raised when Michael cannot hold back temptation and "she" kisses Julie. Julie believes Dorothy is a lesbian, and their friendship is destroyed. The center cannot hold; Michael can no longer maintain the disguise of Dorothy. A sacrifice must be made.

RETURN (ACT III)

The hero must now make the ultimate sacrifice for the greater good. Again, stakes are sufficiently raised to force the hero's final sacrifice of self for community. Will he solve the central problem? What is the **elixir** that is won? These are answered in this final quadrant. In classic comedy, the hero abandons his self-serving ways and reveals his deception. This sacrifice of self for community reaps greater elixirs than he had ever dreamed. Traditionally, the comedy ends in celebration of life and community and often a grand wedding. In *Tootsie*, Michael Dorsey sacrifices Dorothy, revealing his disguise on national television before a live audience. This simultaneously reveals his deception before all of the key characters, including Julie and her father. Initially, the deception destroys his relationship with Julie. But he confesses that the deception has actually made him a better man, resurrecting the hope of love in the final moments of the story. Again, his sacrifice of self grants Michael a greater boon than he had anticipated: Julie, friendship with Julie's father, money for the play, and employment.

Keep in mind, that this is a structural overview. It is not a paint-by-numbers template. Although the *Hero's Journey* paradigm is extremely flexible and adapts to the story you are trying to tell, this general four-quadrant analysis and focus of the *Hero's Journey* as a paradigm for solving the central problem is fairly consistent in successful story-telling. Our hope is that you will refer to this and the Appendix that details the classic twelve story stages as you explore the following comic structures.

COMIC STRUCTURE 1 – THE FISH-OUT-OF-WATER

The **"fish-out-of-water"** is any story that focuses upon placing the main character (the "fish") into a world that is out of his or her element ("out of water").

The fish-out-of-water is the most common of comic structures. It thrives on contrasts and opposition, and is therefore often the easiest story structure to see the comic potential, and the easiest to pitch. A simple way to brainstorm "fish" ideas is to simply ask "what if?" followed by putting someone or something in a situation or environment that is opposite or against their nature.

- What if a desperate, out-of-work actor dressed up as a woman to get an acting job on a soap opera? (*Tootsie*)
- What if a little girl finds herself in the world of the monsters that inhabit her closet? (*Monsters, Inc.*)
- What if a little boy wished to be big — and his wish came true? (*Big*)

- What if an innocent gardener sees the outside world for the first time, and becomes a chief government advisor? (*Being There*)
- What if an FBI agent in denial of her femininity had to disguise herself as a beauty pageant contestant to stop a murderer? (*Miss Congeniality*)

AUDIENCE EXPECTATIONS

Much of the popularity of this "fish" structure is the audience delight in seeing someone often at complete odds with the problem or world they've entered. The comedy rises from the fish trying to cope with the special world that contrasts — often in direct opposition — with the hero's ordinary world. The audience should wonder "who will win?": the fish, or the forces of the special world.

CATALYST FISH VERSUS WOUNDED FISH

There are two general types of fish heroes: the catalyst and the wounded.

The **catalyst fish** (Axel Foley in *Beverly Hills Cop*, Hawkeye Pierce in *M*A*S*H*, Ferris Bueller) doesn't change much during the course of the journey, but his or her "trickster" essence (breaking conventions and rebelling against "SOB") forces change on the special world he enters.

The fish often seeks the special world to solve an external or physical problem. Axel needs to solve his friend's murder. Hawkeye is drafted. Ferris Bueller wants to take the ultimate day off from school. And in so doing, his comic perspective, or essence that defines him in his ordinary world, is seen initially as forbidden by the special world, but soon becomes a special power that promotes change in others. This is the heart of the catalyst fish's journey. The special world grows or transforms because of the fish's presence.

The **wounded fish** (Judy Benjamin in *Private Benjamin*, Josh in *Big*, Amélie in *Amélie*) discovers that the special world can heal a wound that may or may not initially have been consciously known by the fish. The "wound" is usually internal (a search for independence, self-esteem, redemption, or love). Because these are internal goals, they are often not consciously realized. Tackling an external goal may initially place the wounded fish into the special world, and from this new perspective the fish becomes conscious of the wound that must be healed.

Amélie discovers a treasure in her apartment, a box of boyhood memories hidden by a previous occupant. Her external goal is to return the box. But on this journey of becoming a guardian angel to others, she realizes her own need for love.

In *Big*, Josh is a bit more conscious of his wound. Initially he wants to be big, but upon entering the special world of bigness (i.e., adulthood) he learns to love his childhood, and be patient to grow at his own pace.

The fish's worst fear realized can be the ticket to greater rewards in the long run. In *Private Benjamin*, Judy lives her worst fear in boot camp: this is the wrong army. But then after her painful initial tests of waking at the crack of dawn and marching at night in the rain, her parents arrive to take her back. From this new perspective, Judy realizes how stifling her ordinary world was. She wants to stay. And her story is no longer about a stuck-up princess in the army, but a journey of finding one's true self.

Other characters may be transformed by the actions of the wounded fish and his or her unique perspective; however, the heart of the wounded fish's journey is that the fish transforms because of the special world that has been entered. The wounded fish's growth is the story's primary character arc.

These story types are not exclusive. Certainly powerful comedies have been written that use a hero who is wounded <u>and</u> a catalyst.

Gender-bending comedies (*Tootsie, Some Like It Hot, Mrs. Doubtfire, Victor/Victoria, All of Me*) are so satisfying because the reversal of roles gives us outlandish visual comedy. The hero-in-drag undoubtedly causes change in others. In *Tootsie*, Michael Dorsey as Dorothy Michaels gives the daytime drama a strong woman's role, increased ratings, and he gets a couple of potential suitors to boot. But entrance into this gender-switching special world forces the hero to come to terms with both the masculine and feminine sides — and indeed becomes a better person by journey's end. *Miss Congeniality* and *Back to the Future* are additional strong examples of this dual fish-out-of-water story.

THE FISH IN LOVE

One valuable way to view a romantic comedy is essentially as two fish being thrown "out of the water" into the world of romance. Both potential partners are wounded on some level in that they are seeking internal fulfillment and wholeness through love. In the majority of romantic comedies, success is determined by the ability of the lovers to adapt to their new shared fishbowl otherwise one or the other "fish" will jump. A strong catalyst lover may enforce their world to success-fully win love in the end as we see in classic screwball (*Bringing Up Baby*), or turn the potential love away with the tragic catalyst fish fated to find love his way (*Annie Hall*). (See "Comic Structure: Romantic Comedy.")

THE COLLISION OF THE ORDINARY AND SPECIAL WORLDS

The foundation of the fish structure is contrast. The writer should explore the contrast of the fish's ordinary world (what is the fish's natural element) and the special world of the story that the fish must enter (the "out of water"). The greater the contrast of these two worlds, the more potential for comedy through collision.

88

The story concept may support a collision of polar opposites. In *Beverly Hills Cop*, Axel comes from the mean, violent, poor streets of Detroit. He enters the special world of posh, clean, rich streets of Beverly Hills. The polarities are further explored in Axel's character. He breaks the rules, and will even use tactics deemed insubordinate, in order to solve the case. In contrast, The Beverly Hills Police Department is by-the-book. The comedy arises from this collision of polar opposites, as Axel tries to manipulate this special world to serve his needs. And the special world desperately tries to maintain its efficient establishment in response to Axel's inability to play by the rules, resorting to tricks, disguises, and when necessary, in-your-face chutzpah.

The fish structure can be based upon putting your hero in the worst possible situation. Don't make it easy for your hero. Instead, ask yourself what is the worst possible situation in which I can place my hero? In *Back to the Future*, Marty McFly (Michael J. Fox) isn't simply a teen sent back in time. He is sent to the 1950s, and the very time and place of his parent's fateful meeting that cemented their relationship. Marty disrupts this moment, and compounds the problems that he must solve. He not only has to get back to his normal time, but he has to get his parents back together again, or he will no longer exist.

Your story's contrast can be based on a collision of your fish's wish-fulfillment and worst fear. Your hero may pursue the special world to fulfill the greatest wish. In *Big*, Josh's greatest wish of being big comes true. But you can't make it easy for your fish hero. You have the opportunity to put your hero through hell, by creating their worst fear realized. Josh's initial entrance into his special world of bigness is painful. His mother believes he's an intruder and runs him out of the house. He must then learn to survive as an adult in New York City: finding a sleazy hotel room in the worst section of Times Square, securing a job for money. In *The Waterboy*, Bobby Boucher (Adam Sandler) is granted his greatest wish: to play football. But this pursuit of wish-fulfillment collides directly with his mother's ironclad refusal to let him play the sport. His pursuit of his greatest wish (football) must now be juggled with his counter-action of avoiding his greatest fear (mother's wrath).

In *Back to the Future*, Marty doesn't willingly enter his special world of the 1950s. He mistakenly goes back in time when he is fleeing Doc's murderers. But once he goes back in time, he confronts a double-dose of worst fears. He not only breaks up his parent's first encounter, but playing out the worst of Oedipal fears, Marty becomes the new target of his mother's love.

COMMITTING TO THE SPECIAL WORLD

The threshold or moment of committing to the special world must be monumental. Something incredible happens to makes them commit to this extraordinary world:

In *Beverly Hills Cop*, Axel receives the call to adventure: his friend's murder. At the crime scene, his supervisor suggests that it was a hit and he has to stay out. But Axel's sense of responsibility to his dead friend makes him lie to his supervisor and take a "vacation" to Beverly Hills.

In *Back to the Future*, Marty McFly witnesses Doc Brown's murder and barely escapes in the DeLorean time machine and back to 1955.

In *Private Benjamin*, Judy's husband dies on their wedding night and she soon has no sense of life alone — leaving her vulnerable to the seduction of an army recruiter.

In *Splash*, as a child our hero falls off a ferry boat and is saved by a mermaid. Years have passed, but the impact of this encounter has left its mark on Madison the Mermaid. She goes searching for her man.

THE FISH'S SPECIAL POWER

Contrast can be established by the fish's character. Specifically, what character traits and perspectives make the fish unique? And how can the character's comic perspective collide with the special world that needs to be entered?

The character could be the anti-establishment trickster who collides with a rigidly structured establishment (Axel Foley in *Beverly Hills Cop*, Hawkeye Pierce in *M*A*S*H*). Or the fish's ordinary life may be enough to conflict with the proper ways of succeeding in the special world. In *Miss Congeniality*, Sandra Bullock plays an FBI agent who rarely spends time with her feminine side, preferring fast food, and lounging around without a care about how she looks. In order to crack the case, she must pose as a beauty pageant contestant — a special world where looks, manners, and poise are everything — everything she is not in her ordinary world.

This comic perspective is extremely important in the fish story. The aspect or trait of the fish's character not only threatens the operations of the special world, but it also has the potential to be the special power needed to succeed in the special world. This special power may indeed be the elixir that can transform and heal the special world.

These powers may be seen initially as subversive by the special world. In *Harvey*, Elwood P. Dowd (James Stewart) is deemed crazy because he can see an invisible rabbit, Harvey. But by the story's end, the ability to see the rabbit becomes a goal that is pursued by all.

The Beverly Hills Police initially refuse Axel Foley and attempt to suppress his trickster tactics. But as the stakes of the story rise, Axel's subversive powers start winning allies within the department. These allies become key members of the trickster's hero team that ultimately solves the case. And in the end, Axel even earns the respect of Lieutenant Bogomil.

In the light of the ordinary world, the fish's unique perspective of life may seem very unobtrusive and, well, ordinary. But seen through the refraction of the special world, indeed the fishiness becomes a special power that heals. And the fish himself is seen as a special being. The common trickster, clown, or fool is elevated to the Holy Fool, a personage whose innocence is acknowledged as graced by God.

In *Being There*, Chance (Peter Sellers) is a gardener who has been isolated from the rest of the world. His comic perspective has been created by a lifetime of gardening and watching television. Upon the death of his employer and protector, Chance decides to leave his home and journey into the outside world. But his innocence and naiveté are seen as special powers in the "real" world. His matter-of-fact observations of gardening are interpreted as important metaphors for the state of health of the country. The people of the special world elevate this holy fool to public prophet.

In *Big*, Josh enters the adult special world "big" only in size. He still holds his childlike perspective of life (and his computer talents). These seem pretty harmless and hardly elixirs. Yet, within the special world, these are indeed special powers that help him secure a job and excel in a toy company. One of the most memorable moments in *Big* is the FAO Schwartz scene, when Josh reveals his childlike powers to the president of the toy company, and two "children at heart" perform a duet on a giant piano keyboard. Josh is simply pursuing his child's heart, but the president acknowledges his special powers with a promotion to VP of Product Development.

THE FORCE OF OPPOSITION MAY BECOME A KEY MENTOR

Upon entering the special world, the fish will need to know the rules of the special world and what is acceptable and unacceptable behavior. Often we see this played out with initial tests. The fish, trying to survive with his or her comic perspective, is repeatedly squelched by threshold guardians and other forces of opposition.

If the fish is tenacious and deceptive enough, the opposition will be pushed back and may even, as in Hawkeye's case in *M*A*S*H*, be forced to leave. Failing to kick Hawkeye out of the army, Major Burns leaves the 4077th in a straitjacket. Hawkeye's strength of comic perspective is an important theme of that story. The individual must triumph in a world where war is hell.

In the stories of wounded fish, initial forces of opposition can become important mentors that help the transformation and healing of the hero. In order to commit to her special world of becoming a beauty pageant contestant, Gracie Hart (Sandra Bullock) must first pass the scrutiny of Mr. Vic (Michael Caine). He successfully transforms her *physically*, but success of her inner journey will be the reclaiming of her femininity. He helps guide this as well becoming an important mentor within the special world. And despite conflict, in the end the two win mutual respect.

Marty McFly (*Back to the Future*) loses his first mentor at his journey's threshold. He witnesses Doc's murder by terrorists. Marty now finds himself in the 1950s, with barely the knowledge of how to work the time machine. Luckily, Doc had programmed the time machine to travel to his banner day, the day he formulated his time travel theory. Deposited in this special world, Marty must find Doc Brown of the 1950s, and convince him to help. Initially a threshold guardian, Doc becomes an important mentor within the special world to facilitate Marty's return.

If the fish is to succeed in his journey, he must first conquer the "out-of-water" special world. Key allies may be won in the depth of the journey. These help the success of the journey. The most important allegiances can happen when the fish is overcoming the story's central ordeal. Axel continues to break the rules of the special world, and literally drags Detective Rosewood (Judge Reinhold) to the warehouse lair of the bad guys. Axel is caught and held at gunpoint (Ordeal), but Rosewood saves him, finally believing that Axel was right all along. Overcoming this ordeal, Rosewood begins to take on Axel's trickster powers. In like fashion, Miss Congeniality wins the respect of her fellow beauty contestants.

93

EXERCISES:

1. What type of fish are you exploring? A catalyst fish that primarily transforms others? Or a wounded fish that will be transformed the most during the course of your story?

2. Is there sufficient contrast between your ordinary and special worlds to offer comic potential? Is there a feeling that your fish is in collision with the special world of your story?

3. What is your fish's greatest wish and worst fear? Can these be pursued or confronted in the "out-of-water" special world?

4. How does your fish learn the rules of the special world? Is it by trial and error? Does an inhabitant of the special world rise as a key ally or mentor to assist the journey?

A SELECTION OF FISH-OUT-OF-WATER COMEDIES FOR FURTHER STUDY:

The majority of comedies can be seen as "fish-out-of-water" but the following are some good examples for further exploration:

Amélie
Back to School
Being There
Beverly Hills Cop
Big
Dave
Doc Hollywood
Ghost World
The Jerk
Liar Liar
Monty Python's Life of Brian
Miss Congeniality
Never Been Kissed

The Nutty Professor
Private Benjamin
Splash
Trading Places
The Waterboy

GENDER-BENDING FISH

All of Me
Mrs. Doubtfire
Tootsie
Victor/Victoria

TIME AND DIMENSION TRAVELLING FISH

Austin Powers: International Man of Mystery
Back to the Future
Bill and Ted's Excellent Adventure
Honey, I Shrunk the Kids
Kate & Leopold
Sleeper
Time Bandits
Who Framed Roger Rabbit?

COMIC STRUCTURE 2 – ROMANTIC COMEDY

Does **romantic comedy** still sell in an era of divorce and cynicism? You bet it does. Love is the most universal and identifiable of needs, especially for audience members teen through adult. From the most bitter divorcée to the most naive teenager, everyone wants to believe they will find someone who will accept them as they are. That is why we find some level of love — seeking love, winning or losing love, tempted by love — in the majority of cinema stories told. Not just in comedy, but in all genres.

95

Many comedies may have a touch of romance. The love sought may be a sub-plot or added elixir that is discovered or won during the course of the film or journey (*Big, Tootsie, The Graduate*). In this chapter, we focus on the characteristics of the romantic comedy genre. The structure whose purpose is to celebrate the journey of the heart and the elixir of love won despite all odds.

The stories of romantic comedy can be divided into two categories:

1. The search for one's true love (sweet romance) — the hero and/or heroine are wounded without love, discover potential love and try to win it (*Say Anything, When Harry Met Sally, Pretty Woman*).
2. The recommitment to love (marriage comedy) — a relationship (marriage, engagement, or other promise of commitment) is fractured, and the lovers part seeking new love only to come back and recommit to the original relationship, (*The Awful Truth, 10, Desperately Seeking Susan*). Or the relationship is threatened by an external problem (*Adam's Rib, Father of the Bride*).

These are general categories and indeed can be woven together and played with depending upon your story. *Sleepless in Seattle* uses both structures. Annie's story is a search for true love. Sam's story is a recommitment to the power of love. Yes, he's a widower but the death of his wife has shattered his belief in finding love again, and yet, this journey helps him recommit to that romantic notion that true love can be found again.

In another variation, *My Best Friend's Wedding* can be seen as a recommitment romantic comedy. Julia Roberts wants to recommit to the agreement she made with her best friend. And she enters the journey hell-bent on thwarting his wedding and winning him for herself. She doesn't succeed, and the audience, for the most part, agrees with the outcome, wanting to see the wedding go through.

Let's take a look at the story beats that are seen in the traditional form of these two story types.

The Search for True Love

1. Hero is revealed as unfulfilled in life. He or she may not be consciously aware of the inner need to find love to help heal. Perhaps the hero is obsessed with another goal (either an unfulfilled relationship or work) that is taking away any energy or potential commitment to love.
2. The hero confronts the potential love interest. Often this is called the "cute meet" — some unusual encounter that sets the stage for potential romance, and suggests the obstacles that must be overcome if love is to be pursued.
3. The love is pursued, against obstacles that keep the lovers separated. Often the greatest obstacle is a deception created by one or the other lover to get them closer together, or place one lover in a favorable position in the eyes of the potential mate.
4. Obstacles are finally overcome and love is discovered, but true love may still be veiled by deception or sacrificed for another cause.
5. Often the deception has been revealed and miscommunication separates the lovers. The lovers realize with this separation or "death" of love that love is the most important thing worth fighting for. This launches the "chase" to win love.
6. The "chase of the heart" sets one lover fleeing after the other before it is too late. A ticking clock has been set (one of the lovers is leaving town, or going to get married to the wrong person).
7. Love is won, often requiring both to reveal their true feelings.

The Recommitment to Love

1. The relationship is failing. Love is lost. Love needs to be re-found elsewhere. For example, one of the partners may

97

be going through a mid-life crisis, or a bigger problem is getting in the way of their relationship. (In *Adam's Rib* two married lawyers find themselves trying the same case from opposing sides.)

2. One or both in the relationship decide to go their separate ways.

3. They pursue a new love. Jealousy may rear its green head as a major conflict, as the respective lovers must deal with rivals standing in the way of recommitted love. Seeing our old flame entangled in new arms of love can be a death moment that forces us to fight for that love.

4. Also, in the depth of this journey, one of the lovers may try to win back the old love by trying to transform him or herself into the perceived "ideal" love that is now being pursued.

5. They find this new love, but it isn't as they had hoped.

6. The "chase of the heart" sends one lover racing to recommit before it is too late.

7. They return to claim the original relationship.

DISTANCE IN THE JOURNEY OF LOVE

"Absence makes the heart grow fonder," says the cliché. And it does. Absence is a metaphor for distance in romantic comedies. Distance can seem like death to a lover longing for the gentle touch and whispers of a life mate. And this distance can make the lover decide whether love is worth the effort. "Distance" in romantic comedies can be seen from different levels and perspectives.

"Opposites Attract." Another cliché, true. But what more entertaining way to bring potential lovers together than through contrast. After all, romantic comedy is a celebration of love triumphing over reason — i.e., overcoming all obstacles. So, let's establish our lovers divided, "opposites" in some way, from two different ordinary worlds. And then the audience is left wondering how they are ever going to find love.

Distance can separate our lovers in several ways:

Physical Distance. In *Sleepless in Seattle*, Annie lives in Baltimore, Sam lives in Seattle. Physical distance can also be an alternate universe, reality, or time. (*The Purple Rose of Cairo* shows a young woman literally escaping into a motion picture to live her romantic ideal; *Kate & Leopold*, a time-travel romance starring Meg Ryan and Hugh Jackman, uses a century to distance its lovers.)

Class or Cultural Distance. Screwball comedy played off the rift between the "haves" and the "have-nots," showing a woman of high society trying to win a working-class man (*My Man Godfrey, Bringing Up Baby*). Or the runaway heiress stumbling upon unsuspected love (*It Happened One Night*). And the fairy tale romance shows the girl of "ordinary" means or lower class status finding her prince (*Pretty Woman, Mighty Aphrodite*).

Age Distance. A younger lover finding an older mate (*The Graduate, Harold and Maude, Tadpole*). Hollywood convention often has the older man finding love with a pretty young thing, but these stories can explore the other side of the coin: a young man finding love with an older woman.

Professional Stature. Including employer/employee romances. Professional obligations are usually a major obstacle for these lovers, such as conflict of career over relationship/marriage (*Sabrina, His Girl Friday, Broadcast News, Working Girl*).

Distance of Perspectives. The lovers may see the world very differently, and this collision of perspectives is the distance they ultimately must overcome. In *Annie Hall*, Alvy Singer is paranoid, obsessed with death, and fixed in his New York-is-an-island, angst-ridden world. In contrast, Annie Hall is free spirited, living in a world in transition (with a singing career on the horizon). The potential lovers may be on different sides of a specific issue. Addressing this issue is what brings the two together, and at odds (*American President, You've Got*

99

Mail, Heaven Can Wait). In *Speechless*, Geena Davis and Michael Keaton work for opposing political parties during a presidential election. Contrasting perspectives of love could be the chasm that must be crossed. In classic musical comedy (*Guys and Dolls, Annie Get Your Gun*), a song can reveal each lovers' perspective of love. This effectively delineates the distance the lovers will have to cross. Something will need to help bridge this distance, whether one lover realizes that the initial perspective was unachievable or perhaps naïve.

Distance of the Journey Taken. The distance can be seen as the physical and emotional distance one lover needs to travel from his or her ordinary world. In Blake Edward's *10*, Dudley Moore, in the throes of mid-life crisis, seeks Bo Derek, a perfect 10 he has seen from a distance. In his carnal pursuit, he separates from home and wife (Julie Andrews), but the physical and emotional distance from his ordinary world makes him realize that true love is more than young physical beauty. He recommits to his wife, and a healed ordinary world.

SACRIFICING OUR ORDINARY WORLD FOR LOVE

The distance that is established between the potential lovers helps separate their respective ordinary worlds. And for true love to be found, this distance must be bridged in some way. This involves sharing, sacrificing, or perhaps disguising our ordinary world to avoid the greatest fear of refusal.

- The lovers can learn to share their respective ordinary worlds, and the relationship with all of its trials and ordeals is shaped from this mutual sacrifice.
- One or both of the lovers can try to disguise the ordinary world to best fit the perceived ordinary world of the potential mate. This comic deception will need to be exposed. This exposure may ruin the relationship, or perhaps reveal a deeper, more "true" love.

100

- One or both of the lovers try to force his or her ordinary worlds upon the other. Without any flexibility, the relationship is doomed to die. In Screwball, we often see the trickster woman slowly but surely destroying her target's ordinary world, until the exhausted hero accepts the only thing that is left — her love.

MENTORS AND CONFIDENCE ALLIES

Everyone seems to be an expert about two things in life: writing a screenplay and winning a heart. Seriously, people freely give advice about love and can serve as mentors of love. And we, the romantic fools that we are, seek guidance from many types of mentors. We seek advice from buddies who swim the singles stream, and from our parents who are happily married. But we also seem to get aspirations and inspirations of true love from books, movies, songs, celebrity weddings, fairy tales, anything that may give us memories of a first or past true love. Beware, some of these may be false mentors, or idealized memories, representing a love that cannot be attained. And revealing the true "face" of that mentor may be part of the lover's journey.

Another key character we see in romantic comedy is the **confidence buddy**. This person is our romantic hero's best friend who listens to the lover's deepest desires and frustrations. Often these characters are described as reflective characters. The term "confidence buddy" is more apt. The character serves a dual role for the potential lover. He is someone the lover can confide in, revealing his deepest, darkest thoughts. Additionally, the confidence character offers a confidence booster to the lover to pursue the journey of the heart.

George Downes (Rupert Everett) epitomizes this character in *My Best Friend's Wedding*. He offers the shoulder for Julianne to cry upon. But he also pushes Julianne, giving her the confidence to pursue her heart, as long as she is being honest. He cautions Julianne against her meddlesome trickster ways, cluck-clucking in disapproval.

Carrie Fisher and Bruno Kirby portray these characters in *When Harry Met Sally*. Originally set up as blind dates for Harry and Sally, these characters continually remind the audience that Harry and Sally don't really want to be out there in the singles world.

TAKING THE WRONG ROAD BACK

The romantic hero will face two choices at the end of his journey: Commit to the romance or reject it. While most romantic comedies have the traditional guy gets girl, guy loses girl, guy gets girl and lives happily ever after structure, there are also those stories that do not have happy endings. In *My Best Friend's Wedding*, the audience is relieved when Julianne fails in her attempt to break up Mike and Kimmy. The screenplay subverts the traditional expectations of a romantic comedy and the audience realizes that it has been rooting for the wrong character all along.

Similarly, in *Annie Hall*, Annie and Alvy don't get back together again. Alvy resolves his angst by writing a play where he and Annie get together. He realizes that relationships are crazy and irrational and that we're doomed to repeat them. Both of these endings satisfy the audience's need to believe in romance. The audience is reassured that even though romance didn't work out for the protagonist in this story, romances still do work out. Romance enriches our lives and gives us a reason to live.

EXERCISES:

1. Is your story a search for true love or a hidden hunt for recommitment?

2. How are your lovers' ordinary worlds different?

3. What type of distance separates your lovers? How can they overcome this obstacle?

4. In addition to distance, what else can get in the way of your characters' pursuit of love?

5. Does your romantic comedy need a confidence buddy to help the lovers' pursuit?

6. What sacrifice will your romantic hero have to make to find love?

7. Is a comic deception necessary in the attempt to win love? Will this comic deception threaten the central relationship?

A SELECTION OF ROMANTIC COMEDIES FOR FURTHER STUDY

Adam's Rib
Annie Hall
As Good As It Gets
Bull Durham
Bridget Jones's Diary
Broadcast News
Forget Paris
Four Weddings and a Funeral
Funny Lady
Green Card
High Fidelity
His Girl Friday
Keeping The Faith
Moonstruck
My Best Friend's Wedding
My Man Godfrey
Notting Hill
Pretty Woman
Romancing The Stone
Runaway Bride
Say Anything
Shakespeare in Love
Sleepless in Seattle
Speechless
The Sure Thing
Sweet Home Alabama
The Wedding Singer
While You Were Sleeping
Working Girl
You've Got Mail

COMIC STRUCTURE 3 – THE SPORTS COMEDY

There is no finer form of drama than that found in athletic competition. In any sporting event, someone is going to win and someone is going to lose. Athletic competitions result in either the thrill of victory or the agony of defeat. As thus, they serve as a metaphor for life. If you can put aside your selfishness and take one for the team, you will rise to be a leader and a hero. Sport is drama at its simplest and most compelling. *Rocky*, *Brian's Song*, *Rudy*, many films set in the sports genre go beyond great. In fact, *Rocky* and *Chariots of Fire* each won a Best Picture Oscar. The joy and attraction of the **sports comedy** is that it depicts a team that is destined to failure because of comic flaws and infighting. Yet, led by a shape-shifting mentor, this team of lovable losers is able to reign victorious.

Themes in sports comedies tend to restate "It isn't whether you lose or win, but how you play the game." In these stories, the funnies come from the way the characters come together, and confront the opposition (and simply seeing just how awful they really are). Popular themes in the sports genre show a lead character maturing or being educated. These characters take the lessons they have learned from the game and apply them to life. A character may overcome disillusionment or redeem himself. There can be many hybrids in this genre like the buddy comedy (*White Men Can't Jump*), ensemble comedy (*Caddyshack*), romantic comedy (*Tin Cup*), and fish-out-of-water (*Happy Gilmore*).

AUDIENCE EXPECTATIONS

Sports comedy is the comedy of optimism. Sports comedies tell stories of hard work paying off. These stories reaffirm quintessential American ideals like "If you try as hard as you can, you will win." These stories are important because they teach kids how to become part of a team. From an emotional level, the team sports comedy offers a wide selection of losers with which we can identify. These misfits (each with a unique comic perspective) welcome us onto their team. We will invest in their journey, just as if we were playing the game ourselves.

The beauty of a sports comedy is that there is already a built-in audience for the film. The arena of "us" versus "them" in sports competition is universally identifiable. Even an unfamiliar comic world based on a relatively obscure sport (i.e., golf in pre-Tiger Woods days, bobsledding, bicycling, and bowling) can pull in a large audience because of our identification with the thrill of competition.

People of all ages are involved in sports, whether they are affiliated with a school or an intramural league, junior varsity or varsity, professional or amateur. Further, even people who don't actively play sports, either have played sports at one time or enjoy sports on television. And for audience members who failed miserably at sports, sports comedy can vicariously satisfy one's wish-fulfillment to be the loser who somehow, someway, wins the game.

Some critics look down on sports comedies because the endings don't leave much room for surprise. Someone is going to win and someone is going to lose, right? However, when it's done well, the sports comedy can exceed expectations by keeping the suspense until the end. "Will they win?" becomes "There's no way they can win" — and surprisingly turns into: "Oh my God, I think they're gonna win!" Even though we're talking comedy, a good story will have a theme wherein perhaps the team wins something more substantial than the game. Both of our primary sample films for this chapter, *The Bad News Bears* and *Slap Shot*, avoid the "Hollywood" ending. They explode cliché and go for surprise. One ends in loss, the other ends in anarchy. Both are satisfying, successful endings, granting bigger payoffs to the audience than a championship victory or defeat. The filmmakers of *The Bad News Bears* wring every ounce of suspense out of their movie

106

and hold us until the very last out. Alas, the Bears lose the game, but these losers have somehow salvaged victory from the depths of defeat, earning self-esteem and respect. So, let's pick a sport and build a team of lovable losers.

DEFINE YOUR ARENA

There is a broad canvas for sports comedies. Obviously, the most popular sports are easier to sell, but the underlying theme of successful sports comedies is the "underdog triumphs." And this can be conveyed and understood by an audience despite the popularity of the sport. A story involving an unusual or obscure sport may be more compelling then a retread of a misfit's road to the Super Bowl. Choose your sport — from archery to curling, motocross to jousting. Any sport can be considered for your story's arena.

Of course choosing a sport that has limited audience awareness may mean that you'll have to spend more time setting up and establishing the rules of the sport. If you choose the arena of football, for example, there's a huge audience already well aware of the rules of play. You won't have to establish much for the audience to understand what's happening. However, if you pick an obscure sport like squash or curling, you'll probably need to add some entertaining exposition to help the audience understand the comic arena.

An effective way to do this is to put in a character who may not know much about the sport in the first place. This character will need to be taught the intricacies of the sport through a mentor figure. *Cool Runnings* uses this technique. After Jamaican track star, Derice, has a disastrous spill during his qualifying race for the summer Olympics, he is desperate to get into <u>any</u> Olympic sport at any cost. Enter bobsledding, a loophole that helps him realize his dream. Irv (John Candy) is the mentor character that helps Derice realize his dream.

But you can take your time in establishing the arena, as long as it's engaging, visual, and funny. You are transporting the audience into the special world of the sport. And the audience will want some insight into the particular sport, especially the unfamiliar sport (e.g. "Why do people play it?" "What makes them tick?"). Professional athletes are celebrities in their own right, and audiences get a vicarious thrill from looking into an athlete's special world.

SPORTS AS MILITARY CAMPAIGN

The sports comedy has much in common with the combat film (see *Myth and the Movies*). The team enters a new world of competition. It's a world of "us" versus "them." And the "them" — the opposition — is seen as a dehumanized enemy. With opposition often portrayed in outrageous forms of villainy, comic distance is maintained so we can keep our allegiance with the underdogs. The hero team is led by a mentor, the team's coach — a father figure who may serve as councilor and advisor in addition to showing the team how to play and win the game.

FALLEN HERO AS MENTOR

Like the military comedy, many sports comedies will use a central mentor who will lead them to battle. This character is often a wounded hero, a veteran of the sport who will be brought into the fray to relive or resurrect the glory days, or try to heal old battle scars.

In *The Bad News Bears*, Buttermaker is a washed-up minor league pitcher who is now cleaning pools for a living. Coaching a Little League team gives him a chance to earn some extra money and relive his glory days.

Paul Newman's character, Reggie, in *Slap Shot* is a losing player and coach. Even his ex-wife doesn't think he can motivate a team to win. Reg knows he is getting a little long in the tooth to continue coaching and playing hockey. This realization makes him take the opportunity to play goon hockey instead of real hockey.

SETTING UP YOUR LOVABLE LOSERS

It's hard for the team to win if they don't even like each other. The Bad News Bears can barely get through practice without fighting and trying to kill each other. And they're all on the same team. How are they going to bond together and defeat the returning champs at the end of the season?

In *Slap Shot*, the Charleston Chiefs are used to playing in half-empty stadiums, losing, and getting booed by their fans. They're resigned to play bad hockey in a bad part of the country.

Your characters must want to win. However, there will be some incredibly difficult — and funny — obstacles that come between them and winning. And to break this comic distance, you can give your characters identifiable dreams, in addition to the team's goal of victory, to keep the audience rooting until the end.

BUILDING YOUR TEAM

Since the lovable losers and characters are such an essential aspect to the sports comedy, you need to invest significant care in building the team. Be aware of recurring types, and look for ways to break the clichés.

The Bad News Bears gives each team member a unique, comic perspective. There's the overweight Engleberg; the short-fused Tanner; a connected kid, Toby; an ace pitcher, Amanda; a rebel, Kelly; a smart kid, Ogilvie; a wimp, Lupus; big-hearted Rudy; and because the movie was made before the political correctness movement, there are a few stereotypes — a token black Hank Aaron wannabe and two Hispanic kids who don't speak English. Although Amanda, Kelly, and even Tanner emerge as significant characters in the ensemble, all of the characters

109

have brief storylines that touch on their need for a healthy dose of self-esteem. In *Caddyshack*, the wacky ensemble includes: a working-class hero, Danny Noonan; his girlfriend, Maggie; greaser hoodlum Tony; playboy Ty Webb; snobby Judge Smails; his trampy niece, Lacey; nutty groundskeeper Carl; and finally Rodney Dangerfield playing the obnoxious developer, Al Czervik.

Even though these characters have been seen before, *Caddyshack* presents them in novel and hilarious ways. Carl lasciviously watches little old ladies tee off and he grows his own hybrid of bentgrass and sensemilla.

THE COLLISION OF THE UPPER CRUST AND LOWER CLASS

Most of the comedy in *Caddyshack*, *Happy Gilmore*, and *The Longest Yard* comes from the lower class besting the upper class. Everyone loves an underdog, especially when the underdog humiliates and frustrates an arrogant, pompous, and vastly superior opponent. Reducing someone to an infantile state is a popular tool in comedy. Judge Smails (Ted Knight) resorts to childish behavior in the final moments of *Caddyshack*. He pouts, cheats, cries, and is the epitome of a sore loser. The audience delights in seeing this supposedly sophisticated man, a revered representative of the court system, completely broken down at the end of the film.

TRAINING SEQUENCES

A team must be brought together. This takes training. Every sports comedy shows how bad their team really is, so that later the audience will recognize how much progress the team has made. This power of contrast is crucial to the beginning of your story. This is why you first show your character in his ordinary world, so that the audience understands what is so strange and difficult about the special world.

A training sequence is generally soon after the first plot point, or threshold of commitment, of the sports comedy. It establishes hopelessness and calls for someone to rise and rally the team into the special world of winning.

In *The Bad News Bears*, the sequence begins with their pitiful humiliation in the hands of the champion Yankees. Buttermaker compounds this humiliation by forcing the team to forfeit. The team is divided, and Buttermaker begins to see what is most important — the kids need self-esteem. He talks the outfielder out of the tree, and finally in the threshold moment, he tells the team they cannot quit. He forces them back onto the field to practice.

In *Slap Shot*, the ordinary world effectively establishes the team's hopelessness, but one man has a way out. Reg fabricates the story about the team being sold (the comic deception). This event pushes them into the special world. Again, what is the recurring pattern here? The establishment of hopelessness and the crazy deception that pushes them into a special world of competition.

THE SPORTS DECEPTION

A unique aspect of the sports comedy lies in finding an original way to help the underdogs avoid humiliation, embarrassment and, yes, win the game. This requires an element of deception, usually instigated by the mentor. Instead of playing by the rules, or emphasizing "It's how you play the game," the sports mentor will bend the rules to give "us" the advantage. But it's this pursuit to win *at all costs* that usually blows up in the mentor's face.

Good intentions push the mentor to commit to the world of deception and set the stage for his redemption. Buttermaker wants to save face for his team, and avoid the humiliation that will damage the kids' self-esteem. But the mentor is seduced by the goal of winning.

111

Something helps the mentor commit to the special world. Amanda (Tatum O'Neal) agrees to join the team. She brings her great arm and illegal spitball. Later, Buttermaker enlists the juvenile delinquent, Kelly, to single-handedly play the outfield and score the runs. Buttermaker's journey quickly becomes one of winning at all costs.

The mentor often maintains the deception. Keeping important information from the team so as to not crush their hopes.

The Bears were originally created to give the misfits a chance to play the game — because no one else would have them. After the Bears' abysmal pounding on opening day against the Yankees, ending in humiliation and forfeit, the parents want to cut their losses. They even offer Buttermaker a pay-off check. Buttermaker refuses. But Buttermaker keeps this from the kids and sees that they need the team to find some self-esteem.

In *Slap Shot*, Reg needs the team to win in order to thwart the owner's devious plan of intentionally losing to get a bigger tax write-off. This embarrassment motivates Reg to save face for his team. He creates a deception — the rumor of the team being bought by Florida retirees — and he is given a dark call with the inspiration of the Hanson brothers — goon hockey.

NEWSCASTERS PROVIDE EXPOSITION

When the action unfolds, all eyes are on the field. During the game, there is not much room for character development. In the heat of competition, characters don't stop and converse with each other. The sports comedy has an advantage over other genres because it allows commentators to reveal additional exposition. Play-by-play announcers are naturally found in the athletic setting. They can tell the audience — often in humorous ways — what must be going through the main character's mind. These announcers can up the stakes, and fuel suspense, by telling the audience how remote the chances of winning really are.

In addition to commentators providing exposition, spectators can point out how well the hero is doing and comment on character transformation and development. In the opening scenes of *Slap Shot*, the fans heckle the Chiefs and tell the audience just how bad this team really is. Later in the movie, more and more cheering fans root for the Chiefs, and a bus full of boosters travels with the team.

Some of the funnier moments in sports comedy stem from how the players interact on the field. Buttermaker and the loser bench-warmers make acerbic observations from the dugout. Other creative exposition methods and characters can be utilized as well — lovers, ex-wives, parents, and other coaches add to the mix, and provide distinct points of view about how to play the game.

RESURRECTION AND ELIXIR

The resurrection needs a progressive stripping away of the shadow that the mentor now wears. Buttermaker wants to win at all costs. Reg will win by fighting and cheating.

The mentor may need a character to help push them to realize that they're on the wrong journey — they're winning for the wrong reason. The mentor may have taken in a protégé or young hero in the making that initially helped fuel the deception. But soon that same protégé will help the mentor realize he or she is going down the dark path.

Once Amanda is on the team, she discovers a resurrection of her inner journey — to reclaim Buttermaker as a father figure, and even rekindle his relationship with Amanda's mother. As they prepare for the championship game, Amanda realizes that the team will go their separate ways after the season. With this symbolic death looming ahead, she asks Buttermaker to go out with her and her mother after the game. Although Amanda's plea tugs at Buttermaker's humanity, he suppresses it and turns her down, tossing beer in her face. This ordeal divides the two, but begins a process of breaking down the win-at-all-cost shell that has hermetically sealed Buttermaker.

113

In *Slap Shot*, the young hockey star Ned Braden (Michael Ontkean) tries to push Reg to realize that he needs to abandon the journey of goon hockey. But Reg is too deep into the commitment of this special world to change his ways.

One important elixir represents the central character's growth in the sports comedy: the mentor takes his team of losers to the championship game, or final showdown. But during this resurrection, the mentor, and perhaps the entire team, discovers that the journey is about something greater than winning or losing. The elixir is self-respect and reclaiming the joy of playing the game.

The final resurrection of the mentor, the stripping away of the shadow, and the team's return with the elixir can encompass several story beats. Let's look at Buttermaker's and the Bears' resurrection a bit more closely:

At the championship game, Buttermaker begins to see the error of his ways. He lambastes the team in the dugout between innings, and sees in their eyes that he's gone too far — a wonderful moment of simple truth, played out in the eyes of a great comic actor, Walter Matthau. Buttermaker sees the shadow at work in the actions of the Yankees' coach, and realizes how close he is to that rabid fanaticism of winning at any cost. Buttermaker finally lets go, giving everyone a chance to play, even if it means sacrificing the game. And just when it looks like all is lost, the team earns a resurrection comeback with two down. But they lose with the tying run out at home plate. From this great loss, their mentor raises their spirits back up with beer and celebration. They stick their second place paperweight in the Yankees' faces and have a better celebration than the victors.

Thus, by stripping away the shadow mask that is worn within the special world, the wounded mentor is transformed into a better person. And he grants important elixirs to his team. Buttermaker gives Amanda hope of a relationship beyond the ball field. He gives the young kids the power to stand up against humiliation and be a team.

114

THE ELIXIR IS MORE IMPORTANT THAN WINNING

The Bears don't win the championship game, but they are better kids, and a true team, because Buttermaker at last gave them all a chance to play the game. The central goal was no longer winning at all costs, but being a team, and playing to the best of one's ability. And each kid has his or her own little triumph that helps self-esteem.

The elixir in *Slap Shot* is a bit more anarchistic. The championship game has degenerated into a massive brawl, the absurd extreme of goon hockey. Ned refuses to fight, but needs some action to show his own rebellion and reveal the lunacy of where the sport has gone. On center ice, Ned performs a striptease. He succeeds in ending the brawl and making the players question their ways.

EXERCISES:

1. What is unique about the special world of your sport? What is universal? If this is a limited sports arena, what creative ways can you teach the audience about the world?

2. What is your team of lovable losers? Are they unique, yet offer some level of identification to the audience?

3. What is the outrageous deception that forces the team into the special world? Is this known by the team or hidden by someone?

4. Does your team need a mentor? What is he or she after? Is it a wounded mentor in need of redemption? Is he aware of this initially in the journey, or does he have to discover this along the way?

115

5. What aspect of your sports comedy hasn't already been seen by movie audiences? Is there an unusual practice drill, a pre-game ritual, or a unique victory celebration?

6. What are the clichés inherent in your sport? How can you overcome them instead of resorting to them? How can you break these clichés and surprise the audience?

A SELECTION OF SPORTS COMEDIES FOR FURTHER STUDY:

FOOTBALL

Heaven Can Wait
Little Giants
Necessary Roughness
North Dallas Forty
Semi-Tough
The Longest Yard
The Waterboy
Wildcats

BASKETBALL

Air Bud
Celtic Pride
Fast Break
Game Day
Juwanna Mann
Like Mike
MVP: Most Valuable Primate
Space Jam
White Men Can't Jump

BASEBALL

A League of Their Own
Angels in the Outfield
Bull Durham
Major League
Mr. Baseball
Rookie of the Year
Summer Catch
The Rookie
The Scout
The Slugger's Wife

GOLF

Caddyshack
Happy Gilmore
Pat and Mike
Tin Cup

HOCKEY

Slap Shot
Mystery, Alaska
The Mighty Ducks

OTHER

BASEketball
Breaking Away
Jerry Maguire
Kingpin
Ladybugs

COMIC STRUCTURE 4 – THE CRIME/CAPER COMEDY

The **crime/caper comedy** can be one of the most satisfying comic structures for the audience. When done successfully, the crime comedy plays the audience as a mark and surprises them in the greatest of cons. Because the dominant arena in these films is crime, the crime comedies blend thrills with fun. The comedy often comes from smart-mouthed, underdog con artists and criminals, perpetrating outlandish deceptions.

Crime comedies have an increased importance on suspense and surprise. The suspense is focused upon the central conflict. Will the hero/hero team succeed in crime? The stakes are high and this central conflict can be compounded by additional forces of opposition that threaten their success.

The key element of surprise kicks in during the story's final moments. Somehow, hopefully when we least expect it, they succeed.

We are exploring two general types of crime comedy:

> • The comic hero or team pulls off the unbelievable crime or sting.

Examples: *The Sting, Ocean's Eleven*.

> • The comic hero or team fails, realizing that crime doesn't pay.

Examples: *Lock, Stock and Two Smoking Barrels*; *Small Time Crooks*.

Both types of crime comedy have similar story patterns as we'll explore. The story's closing moments distinguish the two. Does the con/caper succeed or not?

AUDIENCE EXPECTATIONS

The crime comedy plays off two of the audience's needs for wish-fulfillment: 1) to break the law and get away with it; 2) to be the underdog and serve revenge or justice to a larger criminal force (mob boss or racketeer).

Audiences enjoy rooting for the anti-hero because the onscreen action helps fulfill our inner desire to break the law. We enjoy seeing how we can dupe the larger societal forces. Remember, comedy often serves as an upstart or revolution against the forces of society that attempt to maintain order. The outlaw serves our wish-fulfillment to break the law and get away with it.

But in successful crime comedies, the target or mark is also on the "wrong" side of the law. Rarely is the victim an innocent, or a person like you and me. Instead, the victim is a villain — almost always a criminal of more devious proportions than our anti-hero. If our heroes are nasty, the villain is nastier, greedier, more wickedly devious, and more bloodthirsty. Having this villainous target helps solidify our allegiance to the hero's team. But watch that the villain isn't over-powerful. The mark must have an Achilles heel — it could simply be greed that leads to the downfall.

These stories engage the audience in a world of cons and deceptions. The entire film is often one large con being played on the audience. We believe the con hero and his team have failed, yet somehow they win with a surprising punch line that dupes the teams' mark as well as the audience with an unexpected, yet satisfying twist.

MOTIVATING THE HERO TO TAKE THE JOURNEY

The hero in a crime comedy is almost always a reluctant hero. The sting or con is going to be so difficult to pull off that almost no one wants to volunteer for a suicide mission. The refusal stage in this journey is so great that the first act of crime comedies frequently require the hero to recruit and train a hero team.

It isn't enough that the hero's team wants to con the villain. They must be sufficiently motivated. The stakes must be raised to push them to take overwhelming risks.

Often, the motivation is revenge. The hero or an ally has been duped by the villain. Or the villain stole something (money, a girlfriend, or wife) from the hero, or even killed an ally or family member close to the hero. Again, the action must raise the stakes enough to rally the hero's team to get revenge.

In *The Sting*, Lonnegan kills Hooker's mentor, Luther. In the recent remake of *Ocean's Eleven*, Andy Garcia steals Clooney's wife while Clooney's character, Danny Ocean, is behind bars.

Be careful that the antagonist's motivating factor isn't so vile that it conflicts with the tone of your comedy. For instance, when Axel Foley's friend is killed in *Beverly Hills Cop*, the violence is so startling that it pulls the audience out of the story. The audience doesn't start laughing again until much later in the story. Be careful when making such a dramatic point, you might not want to cut too deep.

The Coen Brothers take care not to alienate the audience of their crime comedies by using cartoony, over-the-top violence — like the antagonist cheerfully feeding a body into a wood chipper. The audience knows the character is a bad guy who should be feared, but they chuckle at this outrageous sight.

THE IMPORTANCE OF THE HERO TEAM

In the majority of successful crime comedies, a hero's team is built to con the villain. Each member of the team may refuse the call initially; however, the thrill of the con, or the prospects of seeing the downfall of the mark, is sufficient to bind the team. Each member of the hero team ultimately identifies with the main hero's motivation on some level.

Each team member will have his or her own specialty. They have been brought together by a ringleader, who desperately needs the individual skills of each. This ringleader character is often a mentor character, similar in stature and respect as the platoon sergeant of the traditional combat film, or the captain of a team in a sports comedy.

For example, the hero team in *The Sting* includes:

- The experienced leader, mentor, Henry Gondorff (Paul Newman).
- The smooth talker with connections, Kid Twist. His skill: he'll manage the people and the locations to pull it off.
- The wire man, J.J. Singleton. His skill: he knows the inside scoop on the mark, Doyle Lonnegan, and he's an expert at the mechanics of the con games.
- The businessman, Eddie Niles. His skill: he's good at handling money.
- The hero-in-the-making... Johnny Hooker (Robert Redford).

The hero-in-the-making gives the audience a place on the hero's team. This character will ask the questions that the audience would like to ask, because they, too, are learning about this world. This hero-in-the-making is usually taken under the wing of the mentor for part of the journey. In *The Sting*, Johnny Hooker (Robert Redford) is content with small-time cons taught by mentor, Luther. Yet Luther sees talent in Hooker and tries to push Hooker to learn the big con from Henry Gondorff (Paul Newman). It takes Luther's murder to propel Hooker into the special world of the big con with Gondorff.

A LENGTHY APPROACH MAY BE NEEDED

Since crime capers require very complex set-ups, there is generally room for training and planning sequences as the hero's team prepares an approach to the inmost cave. After they have all of their teammates on board, they will need to make the final preparations and frequently rehearse everyone's participation in the sting. You can take your time with setting up the mechanics of the con. If there is a flaw in your logic, the audience will spot it, and the integrity of your entire story goes out the window. This means that the getaway driver can't suddenly hack into the bank's alarm. Each character's role and responsibilities need to be clearly defined and set up in advance. Any failure in completing their duties should become an obstacle that the team can't just gloss over.

WELCOME TO THE WORLD OF THE CON...

If explored in an interesting way, the world of cons and double-crosses is one that the audience wants to know. Remember your audience will find this world unfamiliar and intriguing. They will want to spend time trying to figure things out, especially if you find engaging visual ways to present the world of the con. This stage also serves another level. The team needs to bring the audience in as a fellow member. This helps serve our vicarious need of empathizing with our anti-heroes, and feeling the stakes of the journey. But this also assists with the surprise punch that often happens at the end of these films. We, too, will be conned by this team, but we shouldn't suspect it. Therefore, the stronger the identification with the players, the greater investment we'll take in their story, the deeper we'll be seduced into the con, and the bigger the payoff in the end.

The team's goal upon entering the special world is to hook the villain or mark. If they overcome the central ordeal, and successfully reel in their mark, the team can now play the con until their revenge is played out. This ordeal raises the stakes for the team. There's no turning back — the alternatives are usually jail or death and neither of those options make for a good ending to a comedy. The ordeal or battle provides an opportunity for the talents of our team to shine. This gives the audience false hope that the hero team can indeed succeed.

In *The Sting*, Gondorff out-cheats Lonnegan in a game of poker. Hooker (disguised as Gondorff's right-hand man, Kelly) enlists Lonnegan's help in bringing Gondorff down.

In *Ocean's Eleven*, Saul Bloom (Carl Reiner) hooks Terry Benedict (Andy Garcia) by posing as a wealthy high roller who wants his priceless emeralds stored in Benedict's vault. Once Bloom's emeralds (and the acrobat hiding in their case) are ensconced in the vault, the sting is on and the game must be played to the conclusion.

This level of commitment uncovers other outside forces that are after the target or the con hero in some way. These outside forces threaten to reveal the crime in the making and need to be dealt with. In *The Sting*, Detective Snyder wants to get Hooker for passing counterfeit money. He chases Hooker throughout the story, upping the suspense as he gets closer and closer.

THE SURPRISE PUNCH LINE

The outside forces can be legitimate obstacles threatening the success of the crime or con. The audience is fully aware of Detective Snyder's threat and wonders how the team will overcome it. Other forces may seem like legitimate threats, but are part of the team's con. The limited information given the audience makes these threats real in the world. We believe these forces will destroy the plan if the team doesn't deal with them. What the audience doesn't know is that these forces have been created by our team as part of the con. In *The Sting*, the FBI is part of the con. To the audience, they fit this world's logic as a viable threat. But the FBI is an important element of the con to get Snyder off their trail, and successfully complete the sting. Unaware of this deception, we (and Snyder) see Hooker crumble under the FBI's pressure to bring down Gondorff.

The surprise element is the payoff in the story's final moments. In *The Sting*, the FBI's interruption of the final sting was Gondorff's plan. And the FBI's involvement is essential to complete the sting. The FBI bust forces Snyder and Lonnegan out of the scene, both marks believing that Hooker and Gondorff are dead and Lonnegan's money confiscated.

In *Ocean's Eleven*, the surprise outside force is Saul Bloom's heart attack. The audience doesn't know he's faking it and feels that the con might be lost, despite the best efforts of the hero team.

In *Lock, Stock and Two Smoking Barrels*, outside forces want the same money that the team wants. These are all legitimate threats that raise the stakes of their planned crime. However, a relatively small story element — the antique rifles — become the surprise element in the story. They are revealed to be worth much more than anyone thought.

Whatever the surprise element you bring into your story, you need to set it up sufficiently. You don't want to be too heavy-handed because your intended audience is smart. And what was so successful in *The Sting* can quickly become a cliché. A key to breaking the cliché is to make this subplot a logical element of your story's world that works off emotions, motivations, and stakes of the story. Again, the FBI is a viable threat — this increases the stakes and makes the audience wonder if Gondorff and Hooker will succeed. In *Lock, Stock and Two Smoking Barrels*, the rifles are established almost as an afterthought. These antiques tempt various characters who want them. This element feeds off of characters' motivation and desire. No one (including the audience) realizes the value of the rifles until the information is discovered in a collector's magazine in the final moments.

COMIC STORIES AND THEIR STRUCTURE

EXERCISES:

1. What is unique about the heist you are planning for your crime comedy?

2. What skill sets will be needed to help the hero plan this heist?

3. Who is your hero's target (the mark)? And are the stakes sufficiently raised to commit the team to the crime?

4. How will the hero recruit members for his hero team?

5. What does the audience and the hero or the mark need to know about the special world of the con? How can this be visually revealed? Can it come out of conflict? Out of trial and error?

6. What are potential forces that can threaten your hero's success?

7. In the center of your story, do you need to hook your target or mark to pull them into the con?

8. Does your story have a surprise punch line in the end? Is there a deceptive way to mislead the audience, but still fits in with the reality of your story's world? Does this deception rise from the growing stakes of the story? Or does it play off of the wish-fulfillment of one of your characters that threatens his or her commitment to the crime's success?

9. What is the message you want to say at the end of your story? And how is this played out by the hero's team (do they succeed or fail)?

125

A SELECTION OF CRIME COMEDIES FOR FURTHER STUDY:

Fargo
Snatch
Harlem Nights
Pulp Fiction
Where the Money Is
Throw Momma From the Train
Reservoir Dogs
Dirty Rotten Scoundrels
The Distinguished Gentleman
Sugar & Spice
Who is Cletis Tout?
Trapped in Paradise
Go
Jackie Brown
Beverly Hills Cop
48 Hours
Blue Streak
Metro
Small Time Crooks
Take the Money and Run
Bandits
Butch Cassidy & The Sundance Kid
Thelma & Louise
Who Framed Roger Rabbit
O Brother, Where Art Thou?
The Big Lebowski
Raising Arizona

COMIC STRUCTURE 5 – THE MILITARY COMEDY

Honor, duty, and patriotism. These themes run throughout war movies like pick-up trucks through country music. **Military comedies**, particularly American military comedies, must walk the fine line of poking fun at these themes without being unpatriotic. You can make fun of the military, but you can't make fun of America or American ideals. Like good black comedy, which shows the positive by accentuating the negative, sometimes a military comedy can actually be patriotic, showing a hero subverting a military clown. Ultimately, the hero will reveal that his disrespect for rules and regulations is how he expresses his right to free speech, showing the audience that the hero is more American and patriotic than the by-the-book military man.

AUDIENCE EXPECTATIONS

How will a fish-out-of-water trickster (Bill Murray, Goldie Hawn, or Pauly Shore) survive in the hardline military world? Will an unlikely hero learn to subvert military authority and come out on top? In military comedies, the answer is — Yes. A misfit hero will find hidden strength and will learn to lead. The hero will call on long-forgotten special powers and motivate his or her platoon to victory. But it's the trickster's unique subversive powers that attract the audience to the military comedy.

THE TRICKSTER HERO

Military heroes are typically tricksters and bombastic con artists. They do not respect or fit into the rigid chain of command. This type of hero is frequently a rebel who refuses to conform, or someone who would otherwise fail in a military environment.

John Winger (Bill Murray) is a lovable, charismatic loser in *Stripes*. He's failing as a New York City photographer and in one day, he loses his job, his car, his girlfriend, and his apartment.

In *Private Benjamin*, Judy Benjamin (Goldie Hawn) is a spoiled princess who has been taken care of her whole life. After her husband dies, she falls for an Army recruiter's pitch about joining an Army with beachfront condos and yachts and is told if she doesn't like it, she can just quit.

In *M*A*S*H*, Hawkeye Pierce (Donald Sutherland) is an unconventional slob who disrespects the military at every turn. He refuses to wear a uniform and is mistaken for a driver by a fellow surgeon reporting to the 4077th.

ESCALATING CLASHES AND COLLISIONS

Most of the comedy with these characters comes from the clash and collision of the trickster's ordinary world meeting the rigid and inflexible special world of the military. Over the course of the story, these heroes will become more familiar with the ways of the military and resort to more and more outlandish ways to denigrate the responsibilities they have been given and abuse the authority figures or officers above them.

John Winger starts off cracking jokes at Sgt. Hulka's expense. In the third act of *Stripes*, he talks his buddy into borrowing (stealing) an advanced new weapon to visit their girlfriends. Naturally, this sets off a chain reaction of conflicts and collisions with authority figures, including a hilarious series of running gags involving two Czech border guards.

Judy Benjamin believes that she can quit the Army anytime she wants. She falls asleep on the bus on the way to boot camp. When the Sergeant asks her to report to duty, she requests a little more sleep. We laugh as Judy is tossed off the bus and opens her eyes to the harsh reality of her new world.

Hawkeye gleefully plays practical jokes on other officers. He turns Frank Burns' Bible-studying house boy into a bartender, makes a medical emergency fit around his golf schedule, and turns Hot Lips' shower into a peep show for the entire camp.

The key for extending the humor in these films is to keep raising the flag higher up the flagpole. You will notice that the authority figure targets in *Stripes* escalate in military rank from Sergeant Hulka to Captain Stillman to General Barnicke. Notice that the filmmakers do not allow Winger to be insubordinate to Captain Stillman or General Barnicke. In fact, those characters rarely act in scenes together. If a lowly enlisted man were to be directly insubordinate to an officer, it would shatter the suspension of disbelief. Officers will confront higher ranking officers and reveal their ineptitude, but the lowly trickster seldom deals with them directly.

Generally, the higher up the food chain, the sillier and more inept the leader. Captain Stillman (John Larroqutte) in *Stripes* is a green leader. He spends most of his time playing Army with toys in his office, peering through a telescope into the girls' locker room, and his critical catalyst moment of ineptitude comes when he orders a soldier to fire a mortar without calculating the coordinates. The errant mortar injures Sergeant Hulka and puts our heroes in jeopardy of having to repeat basic training.

Colonel Thornbush in *Private Benjamin* is portrayed as an egocentric buffoon, who has named a platoon after himself. Major Burns in *M*A*S*H* is a dim-witted, Bible-thumping, incompetent surgeon.

SPECIAL POWERS OF THE HERO

The military comic hero is a fish-out-of-water, floundering in the structured world of the armed forces. We will see this hero flailing, gasping for air, and figuratively dying because he or she refuses to follow the rules of the military world. Despite this potentially fatal flaw, the skills that the heroes have retained from their ordinary world may help them overcome the difficulties they are having surviving in the special world. After they reveal the unconventional tactics that allow them to succeed, they are often rewarded with promotion and given a new-found respect by the military brass.

John Winger uses his charisma and crude songs to motivate his fellow soldiers. When it looks like all is lost, he gives a stirring speech about how Americans got kicked out of every respectable country in the world and emerged as the most ferocious fighting mutts on the planet. The platoon's unusual graduation performance impresses General Barnicke and they are selected to work on the prestigious EM50 project.

In *Private Benjamin,* Judy remembers Gianelli's sexy red underwear. She fashions this non-regulation accessory into an armband disguise, which helps the misfits from the blue platoon capture the red platoon and pass a vital test during the war games. When Colonel Thornbush learns how Judy tricked the red platoon into surrendering, he is impressed by her unconventional thinking and Judy is given a prestigious assignment after boot camp.

Hawkeye's lack of respect for standard military clowns is a running gag in *M*A*S*H.* After embarrassing higher ranking officers Lieutenant Houlihan and Major Burns by broadcasting their lovemaking over the camp public address system, Hawkeye's topper is exposing Houlihan during her shower and sending Burns off in a straitjacket. Later, Hawkeye outwits another military clown in Tokyo who tries to prevent him from operating on a Korean baby.

Notice the contrast in these military tricksters. In *Stripes* and *Private Benjamin,* the trickster's special powers are celebrated, largely for comic effect. In *M*A*S*H,* Hawkeye is forced to use this special power because it is the only way he can do what he believes is right (saving the baby) during this insane time of war.

CROSSING THE THRESHOLD

The threshold moment is a key plot point where the stakes force the trickster hero to commit to the rigid and unbending special world of the military. This moment clearly distinguishes the differences in the two worlds, forcing the hero to contemplate admitting failure and returning to their ordinary world, or striving to be all they can be, and really apply themselves toward military success.

Threshold sequences show the transition from civilian life to military life: getting haircuts, putting on uniforms, and eating in the mess hall. These sequences signify the hero's descent into the special world of the military. Discarding civilian clothes for military uniforms is a figurative shedding of the skin and tells the hero that he will have to abandon his individuality and become part of a team if he is to survive.

Numerous tests abound in this special world. Basic training sequences usually show the military machine breaking down individuals and getting them to put their unit before everything else. Harsh punishment is meted out to those who continue to put themselves before their unit. Every time John Winger puts himself before his platoon in *Stripes*, we see him doing pushups in the rain as Sergeant Hulka stands under an umbrella counting them off. The filmmakers cut to enough of these sequences and the bit becomes a nice running gag.

These tests are not set patterns, but they can be used, depending on the tone of the military comedy you are trying to write. *Stripes* and *Private Benjamin* show the unlikely trickster ultimately becoming the military hero. In *M*A*S*H*, trickster Hawkeye maintains his subversive individuality to reveal the craziness of war. He does not become a military hero in the same sense as Winger and Benjamin; however, he becomes a hero to his ideals — using his trickster powers to do what he believes is right. His threshold sequence is one of stalwart subversion, initiating an escalating series of tests of his trickster tactics versus hard-line military regulations. The weaker authority figures are pushed out of the way, or taken away in a straitjacket, like Major Frank Burns.

MENTOR AS FATHER FIGURE

In most military comedies, the Drill Sergeant serves as a mentor as well as an antagonist. This individual will show the hero that he must ignore the self-gratifying intuition and the skills that got him through his ordinary world. There are new rules in the special world of the military. The mentor must teach the hero to sacrifice his or her individuality for the platoon, and obey orders without question to uphold the military's chain of command. This tough-as-nails bastard provides an additional level of antagonism for the hero. These mentors often doubt that the hero has the discipline or fortitude to make it through basic training. They will challenge the hero at every turn. This character may turn out to have a heart of gold and will rally to the hero's aid after the hero has proven himself fit for military life.

Sergeant Hulka in *Stripes* goes after his platoon and helps rescue them from enemy territory. Drill Sergeant Ross in *Private Benjamin* rewards Judy with paternal approval after she one-ups Captain Lewis. Colonel Blake refuses to discipline Hawkeye because he is the best surgeon in the camp.

These mentors unite the hero team and prepare their charges for the battlefield. However, they can't do it by themselves. At some point, they must step aside.

SACRIFICE OF THE MENTOR

In many military comedies, the platoon leader is sacrificed so that the hero can take responsibility and lead the team. In *Stripes*, Sgt. Hulka is blown up and John Winger must lead his platoon through the ordeal of their graduation exercises.

Even if the mentor isn't killed, they must be eliminated so the hero can assume power and succeed on their own. After the hero succeeds, there may be a scene where senior officers grudgingly approve of the fresh new perspective that the hero has brought into the military environment. After the hero makes his/her heroic sacrifice, he learns what it means to be part of a team/unit.

When the mentor is a force of antagonism, the trickster hero must sacrifice them, pushing them out of the way using their unique tactics. Hawkeye drives Frank Burns to insanity and renders Hot Lips into submission.

Judy Benjamin one-ups Captain Lewis by enlisting her squad to send off Captain Lewis with a "blue shower." In these stories, the mentor as a force of antagonism is sure to rear the head of revenge.

REWARD AFTER GRADUATION

In many military comedies, the hero is given a reward after completing his training. The reward celebrates the hero's transformation and subsequent success in the special world. They've succeeded in the special military world, but they've also maintained their unique trickster perspective, despite the military's intentions to strip them of this powerful reflection of their individuality. This reward allows the hero to rest and recharge his batteries, but it is the calm before the storm. The hero will soon have to lead his troops into battle and face the ultimate ordeal. The reward may give the hero a promotion that will move the story into another arena and up the stakes as the story moves toward its climax.

In *Stripes*, the heroes are given the reward of being assigned to the EM50 project in Europe. This leads them to their ordeal when they accidentally invade Czechoslovakia and have to use their newly acquired military skills.

In *Private Benjamin*, Judy is rewarded with leave in New Orleans. She meets her new love interest, the French gynecologist. Then she gets assigned to the Thornbirds and ultimately winds up being stationed in Belgium to be near her new love. This sets up the central crisis in Judy's special world: military career versus new love.

COMEDIC EXPLORATION OF DEATH

Death is an essential part of military life, yet many people writing military comedies are conflicted about how to portray death. Killing characters that the audience cares about is not funny, and reduces the effectiveness of your comedy. Some military comedies treat death in violent and cartoonish ways. They kill off a minor character in a scene that reveals that character's inadequacy as a soldier. There are two benefits to this. First, death raises the stakes for your hero. No matter how funny the death is, the audience remembers that this fate could befall the hero. Second, a death releases the tension in the audience and primes them for laughter.

Lots of comedic action takes place during training exercises and war games. War games are often utilized to summarize the lessons learned in basic training and foreshadow the skills that the hero will need during their ordeal. War games also provide a safety net of comic distance. The audience can laugh because the hero is only subverting war games and overcoming tests. People aren't dying.

EXERCISES:

1. Why will your character have a difficult time fitting into the special world of the military?

2. What are the special powers of your trickster hero? How can these powers manifest themselves in the tests and ordeals of the military's special world?

3. How are the stakes sufficiently raised for your hero to commit to the military institution?

4. What fresh twist can you put on the sacrifice of the mentor? What if your irascible Drill Sergeant were a woman, soft-spoken, gay, or quoted poetry?

5. Think of potential fish-out-of-water scenarios for a Gulf War hero?

6. What humorous scenes could come from the War on Terror?

A SELECTION OF MILITARY COMEDIES FOR FURTHER STUDY:

Biloxi Blues
Buck Privates
Good Morning, Vietnam
Hot Shots!
Hot Shots! Part Deux
In the Army Now
Jumping Jacks
McHale's Navy
No Time for Sergeants
Sgt. Bilko
Small Soldiers
Down Periscope

COMIC STRUCTURE 6 –
THE TEEN/COMING-OF-AGE COMEDY

Teen comedies celebrate a coming of age, a passage from childhood to adulthood. Often nostalgic, **teen/coming-of-age comedies** can hearken back to simpler times, when life was uncomplicated. These tales can be a celebration of teenage rebellion and anarchy. The most lasting coming-of-age tales offer an identifiable and painful story world that explores the turbulence of adolescence. These stories can be an audience member's most memorable because they can help soothe the anxieties a teen feels at this awkward stage.

Since teens make up the biggest segment of the movie-going public, teen comedies are very commercial. They are often high concept in nature, with a premise that can be summarized in one sentence. In *American Pie*, four high school buddies make a pact to lose their virginity by prom night. *Sixteen Candles* is about a girl whose parents forget her birthday. Coming up with fresh takes on the teen comedy genre is difficult, because teen comedies usually only revolve around two things.

- Hero wants to get a girl/guy
- Hero wants to become popular/gain acceptance

The comedy writer tackling the teen audience should begin by looking within themselves, and tapping their memories and experiences. Try to see the world again through teen-angst eyes. They will unearth a wealth of unique situations and characters with a universal resonance that can effectively touch the emotions and speak for the teen audience.

Compounding the challenge is the fact that the setting is usually limited to school, either high school or college. A good comic writer knows that even the shallow constraints of high school offers an unlimited number of arenas for comic exploration. Characters can be goths or gearheads, heavy metalers or hip-hoppers, stoners or straights. The more defined your comic arena is, the easier the jokes will flow. Character goals can be losing one's virginity, getting a date to the prom, becoming popular. However, there will generally be something bigger at stake.

BASIC CHARACTERISTICS

The hero's journey in a teen comedy offers many layers of conflict and collision. There is often conflict between parent and child, student and teacher/principal, hero and popular crowd, and hero and love interest. Love triangles may also be used to complicate the journey, and fuel surprise and suspense. Obstacles are frequently misunderstandings between characters. There is also inner conflict with the teen coming to grips with growing up. What makes them cool? Why doesn't anyone understand them? What do they have to do to be popular? How will they lose their virginity? This journey toward adulthood usually ends with the elixir of enlightenment. The teen learns that being popular really isn't important, or that the head cheerleader wasn't really the right girl after all.

AUDIENCE EXPECTATIONS

Teen comedies allow us to relive the awkward universal experiences of our own coming of age. The teen will seek these films in order to laugh at the same situations and feelings they themselves may be going through. However, comedy is exaggeration, and exaggerating the hardships of the characters — whether through flaws, miscommunication, deceptions, and even gross-out humor — can help us laugh at the characters on screen. But don't forget that successful teen films have heart. The writer needs to be aware that the audience wants to laugh at the characters, but they also seek characters with which they can identify. Character flaws, identifiable goals, discomfort, pain, and embarrassment can likewise fuel audience empathy. Also, the main character's transformation can be the thread that holds the audience's heart throughout the journey. These teens (and their audience) learn a profound lesson from their experiences, no matter how embarrassing they are. Plus, they usually get a happy ending.

Successful teen comedies will combine elements of black comedy, ensemble comedy, romantic comedy, and fish-out-of-water comedy. Most teen comedies are variations of the romantic comedy where guy meets girl, guy loses girl, guy gets girl again. Teen sex farces show the desperation of the hero to get laid or lose their virginity. The audience can easily identify with their desires and laugh because they have felt the same angst. Ironically, these sex comedies steer away from nudity and/or explicit sexual situations. Today's movie studios want their teen comedies to get a PG-13 rating so they can reach the widest audience possible. Brief nudity is permissible if it's related to the comedy of embarrassment, anything more risqué belongs on the unrated, special edition DVD.

THE ORDINARY WORLD IS LONELY AND FRUSTRATING

Since the goal is love or acceptance, we need to show how lonely and desperate the hero is. In *Sixteen Candles*, Sam is depressed because her family has forgotten her birthday and she pines over a dreamy senior who doesn't even know she's alive.

Jim, the hero of the ensemble cast in *American Pie*, gets caught masturbating and then strikes out with his dream girl, Nadia. It looks like he'll never get laid.

Both of these characters have lonely and frustrating ordinary worlds. What will it take for them to enter the special world of acceptance and an adult relationship? Most likely, they will have to endure a lot of embarrassment, misunderstandings, and frustration in order to receive the elixir of enlightenment.

THE COMEDY OF FRUSTRATION

Teen movies find comedy in sexual frustration. Sex being foremost in a teenager's mind does not always result in clear, logical thinking. Frustration, misunderstandings, and embarrassment will add up to a trifecta of laughs. Remember to use suspense and surprise to string them all together.

Samantha in *Sixteen Candles* has an embarrassing moment when the Geek (Anthony Michael Hall) kisses and climbs on her at the school dance. After he apologizes, she says it's okay. He then tries to climb on her again. She pushes him off and explains that she was accepting his apology, not giving him permission to maul her. After the Geek, a mentor character, advises her on how to approach her true love, Jake, she agrees to do the Geek a favor. She lends him her underwear, so he can win a bet that he placed with his dorky friends. This bit is well set up and will lead to further embarrassment later. This whole sequence stems from sexual frustration, which leads to misunderstanding and culminates in embarrassment.

In *American Pie*, Jim's sexual frustration is a vital part of his ordinary world. He is trying to masturbate to scrambled porn on cable when his mother comes in to say goodnight. Sexual frustration motivates all of the characters in *American Pie* to make a pact to lose their virginity before graduation. Along the way, they each have a lot more frustrating moments that will lead to embarrassment and big laughs for the audience, especially Jim.

THE COMEDY OF EMBARRASSMENT

American Pie delivers raunchy and embarrassing moments that ring true to the teenage sexual experience. Jim's parents catch him masturbating. His Dad walks in on him having relations with a pie. The filmmakers exaggerate this embarrassment when Jim's Dad brings him dirty magazines and talks to him about masturbating. How embarrassing! Who wants that? We've all had those awkward talks with our parents, so we understand them and we can vicariously laugh at the character's discomfort. Then, worst of all, Jim has an embarrassing incident with premature ejaculations and it's broadcast to the whole school. These bits would be considered lowbrow, but the movie has so much heart. Only when all of the characters give up on their pact do they get their rewards. Thus, the teenage sex comedy prepares them for life outside of high school. They are ready to take the next step.

THE COMEDY OF THE GROSS-OUT

Gross-out gags are found in teen comedy and delight the audiences of coming-of-age films.

National Lampoon's Animal House has a great gross-out gag where Bluto (John Belushi) stuffs his face full of food and spits it out all over a bunch of stuffy fraternity and sorority types in the cafeteria. He's imitating a zit. Get it? It's funny because the victims deserve to be taken down a peg. It wouldn't be so funny if it were happening to a likable character.

Gross-out gags abound in *American Pie* and have since been imitated in numerous teen comedies. It is important to remember that gross-out gags are their funniest when an arrogant character gets his just desserts. If the hero is the target, the moment is often more painful and embarrassing than funny.

THE COMEDY OF MISUNDERSTANDING

Misunderstandings can complicate the teen life. These can range from vicious rumors to simple misunderstandings. Deceptions can compound, building suspense and conflict with laughter rising as the hero desperately attempts to correct the misunderstanding. In *Sixteen Candles*, Jake misunderstands Sam's inability to speak to him as loathing. The Geek tries to correct this misunderstanding. However, it is Sam who must ultimately correct Jake's misperception about her.

In *American Pie*, misunderstandings move the second act forward. Vikki hears Kevin tell Jim that he's sick of blowjobs, he wants to get laid. She asks Jessica for a ride home. This misunderstanding gives Kevin a big obstacle to overcome if he is to fulfill his pact.

THE ELIXIR OF ENLIGHTENMENT

In most teen comedies that celebrate our rebellious natures, the anti-heroes are able to use their anarchistic special powers to overcome the consequences of their actions. *Animal House's* Delta House gang turns the homecoming parade into chaos, showing the stuffed shirts of authority, and the rival fraternities, that rebellion grants a better future.

During the journey, our teenage protagonists think they want one thing when what they really get is another. Usually it's something deeper, and more significant. Often this is true love, friendship, or acceptance despite our flaws. *American Pie* uses set pieces to cut back and forth between each of the four protagonists as they struggle to reach their goal of getting laid before graduation. But this isn't their elixir. They realize that this rite of passage wasn't as important as they thought. There are more important things in life, such as their friendship and going to college.

Meanwhile, in *Sixteen Candles*, Samantha survives the ordeal of her sister's wedding and is resurrected when Jake shows up to meet her. She tells him that she doesn't have to go to the reception and he gives her the reward of a birthday cake. He tells her to make a wish; she says she doesn't have to, because it's already come true. She has received the elixir of enlightenment.

EXERCISES:

1. What is your hero after in your teen comedy? What are your character's flaws?

2. What is your hero's greatest fear?

3. How can you embarrass your hero?

4. How can misunderstanding complicate the journey?

5. What unique obstacles does the hero in your teen comedy face?

6. What is the reward your hero seeks and how can you turn that reward into an elixir of enlightenment?

A SELECTION OF TEEN/COMING-OF-AGE COMEDIES FOR FURTHER STUDY

10 Things I Hate About You
American Graffiti
National Lampoon's Animal House
Clueless
Fast Times at Ridgemont High
Ferris Bueller's Day Off
Hairspray
Porky's
Pretty In Pink
Risky Business
Road Trip
The Breakfast Club
The Wedding Singer
Van Wilder
Weird Science

COMIC STRUCTURE 7 – ENSEMBLE COMEDY

The majority of structures we've focused on have dealt with a single comic hero in pursuit of attaining a goal or solving a problem. This defines the central plot, which may have additional subplots of conflicts, but each supporting the main thrust of the story.

The **ensemble comedies** we are exploring in this chapter focus not on one central hero, but a group of characters. Multiple subplots or storylines are woven throughout; they may touch, cross over, and rebound off of other subplots, but the individual story threads are maintained throughout. The power of this type of comedy lies in its ability to show different perspectives, responses, and actions/reactions by various characters within a world.

There are ensemble comedies that bring a hero team together to solve a central problem (see Crime, Military, and Sports Comedies for examples). Ensemble comedies like *Animal House* or *M*A*S*H* deal with multiple plot lines but these dovetail ultimately with the group coming together to solve the problem (to thwart the homecoming parade, or win the football game respectively).

An ensemble can define the dimensions of a specific world, issue, or other source of stimulus. One character may be featured in the comedy (for example, Steve Martin in *Parenthood*), but overall, the ensemble movie is an exploration of a group or issue seen through various points of view. This weaving of subplots and points of view can make the ensemble comedy the most difficult to write. The first thing the writer approaching this form needs to ask is: what is the unifying force or idea of this story?

By its nature, the ensemble film is not framed by one central action; however, we can unify the ensemble in other ways. By characters, place, event, theme, or social issue. An ensemble comedy may focus on one of these unifying forces, but successful ensemble comedies usually incorporate several if not all of them on some level.

ENSEMBLE UNIFIED BY A GROUP OF CHARACTERS

The writer may use the ensemble comedy to explore a group of people, a professional world, or a subculture of society as defined by the people who live in that subculture.

Clerks explores the special world of minimum wage store clerks.

Fast Times at Ridgemont High explores the lives of high school students.

The Royal Tenenbaums explores the family Tenenbaum.

The Big Chill explores the reunion of best friends.

Parenthood explores a family with a common point of view — they're all parents.

Hannah and Her Sisters explores the lives of three sisters and their relationships.

Network explores the ethics, or lack thereof, in the television news business.

In this type of ensemble story, filmmakers bring us into a unique world and entertain us with a journey we wouldn't otherwise take. When done well, these stories serve as anthropological fables, giving us insight into a particular class or subset of people. At the end of an ensemble piece, the audience will feel like they have lived the lifestyle. They are now experts in the field.

Therefore establishing and explaining the rules of your special world becomes critical. Setting up each character's perspective is essential and will help the audience relate to the new world.

Clerks serves as a good example of an ensemble unified by a group of characters. All of these characters work or hang out at a local strip mall. Dante (Brian Halloran) works at the convenience store. His best friend, Randal (Jeff Anderson), works next door at the video store. Dante's current girlfriend, the talkative Veronica, and his ex-girlfriend, Caitlin, come by the store because it's the only place they can talk to Dante. The other two main characters Jay and Silent Bob are drug dealers who hang out in the parking lot. The audience gets the sense that Dante and Randal are bored with their jobs. In fact, Randal insults almost every customer who comes into his store. The filmmaker does an excellent job of placing these characters in a unique world and setting up each character's comic perspective. Dante is bitter that he has been called in on his only day off and gets even more mad when he may miss his hockey game because of work. Randal is so bored at work, he starts wondering how many innocent construction workers were killed in *Return of the Jedi*.

ENSEMBLE UNIFIED BY ISSUE OR THEME

A writer may use several stories or a particular issue to bring a theme or new line of thinking across. Sometimes this theme may not become apparent during the writing of the first draft. Significant introspection may be needed to discover what the writer really wants to say.

Fast Times at Ridgemont High shows us teens trying to act like adults in a teen world.

Hannah and Her Sisters comments on how unpredictable love is.

Parenthood presents the difficulties of parenting from different viewpoints.

The Royal Tenenbaums deals with the issues of family, love, and success.

Several issues run through the movie *Parenthood*. Will Gil (Steve Martin) be able to be a good father and advance his career? Will Helen (Dianne Wiest) get over her first bad marriage and find a personal life? Will Frank (Jason Robards) bail his son Larry (Tom Hulce) out of yet another financial disaster? Will Nathan (Rick Moranis) and Susan (Harley Kozak) separate because Nathan is too rigid with their daughter? Each character has a remarkably different view on parenthood, and equally challenging goals, yet these stories are all tied together with one theme — parenting.

Because each set of characters has a strong perspective on how they parent, the stories are distinct and easy to jump in and out of. In the beginning of the story, all of these characters seem so different that it's hard to believe they are related. By the end of the movie, the audience realizes that even though these characters each have a unique viewpoint, they are all the same: hard-working and earnest parents.

Gil doesn't want to make the same mistakes his father made. Yet his son, Kevin, needs therapy because Gil brings stress home from the office. Gil wants to balance his job and his family, but fears he is only screwing both up. He learns a final lesson from his father when Frank tells him — parenthood never ends!

Helen can't get a personal life because her husband left to have a party and she stayed to raise two kids. Both of her children are going through rough times, Julie with her relationship with Todd, and Garry who needs a father figure.

Meanwhile, Susan wants to teach summer school, so she and Nathan can take a romantic vacation and conceive their second child. Nathan, however, wants to wait five years between siblings to maximize their academic potential.

Larry brings home his son, Cool, because Cool's mother dumped the child on him. "That's a parent!" he foreshadows ironically in a conversation with his father. He will later leave the child with his parents.

146

These four main stories skillfully link the theme of parenthood through a series of subplots featuring an excellent ensemble cast. *Parenthood* is more than the light-hearted fluff it pretends to be.

ENSEMBLE UNIFIED BY EVENT

A significant event may bring the ensemble together. A murder unifies *The Cheap Detective*, *Clue*, and *Gosford Park*. A race brings together the casts of *It's a Mad, Mad, Mad, Mad World*, *Rat Race*, and *The Cannonball Run*. A heist attracts the cast of *Ocean's Eleven* and *Lock, Stock and Two Smoking Barrels*. The time duration of this event may also unify the story. At the end of an ensemble, a minor character or narrator may tie up the loose ends, by telling us what this story was all about.

In *Meatballs*, summer camp brings the ensemble together.

The end of the school year helps unify *Fast Times at Ridgemont High*.

In *The Royal Tenenbaums*, the event is Royal (Gene Hackman) wanting to win back his family and his wife.

A friend's suicide brings the ensemble of *The Big Chill* together.

Ensembles unified by event may be more dramatic than slapstick. They have a strong story structure at their core. Of all of the unifying factors, perhaps event offers the greatest opportunity to explore different tones within the story — one subplot could be more dramatic in tone whereas another storyline could be pure silliness. But ensemble pieces by their nature of offering different perspectives, also offer different tones within one story.

In *The Big Chill*, friends who have drifted apart spend a weekend dealing with their friend's death. Each character reevaluates his/her life and reaffirms the bond they have with their friends.

The Oscar-winning screenplay for *Gosford Park* unifies its cast by having them discover a murder at an English country estate. As the story progresses, we learn that each guest had strong motives for wanting their host dead.

Several important events help structure *The Royal Tenenbaums* and bring about the eventual elixir of family healing and forgiveness. After their rogue father (Gene Hackman) sneaks back into their lives by feigning a terminal illness, he causes total chaos. The family comes together to forgive Royal. Royal helps Richie deal with his failed pro-tennis career and "forbidden" love for his adopted sister, Margot. Although he initially tries to break up Etheline's relationship with Harry, Royal sacrifices all hope of restoring his marriage. Royal gives Etheline (Angelica Huston) the official divorce papers with his blessing to move on with her life and marry Harry (Danny Glover). This act of forgiveness presents a second event that begins to bind the family again — the wedding of Etheline and Harry. Etheline and Harry get married. Richie starts a tennis program. Eli goes to rehab. Margot's play opens for two weeks. The last sibling to hold back his love for Royal, Chaz, is the only Tenenbaum to witness Royal's death from a heart attack. Chaz rides with him to the hospital. Witnessing Royal's death restores father/son love. In a final scene, Royal's funeral takes place at dusk. No one speaks. Royal's gravestone is how we learn what the movie is about. It reads: "Royal O'Reilly Tenenbaum — died tragically rescuing his family from the wreckage of a destroyed sinking battleship."

UNIFICATION OF PLACE

Place can help define the world and the ensemble that lives in that world. But that place may be an uncomfortable one for the ensemble to inhabit.

Clerks is primarily set at the convenience store.

Fast Times at Ridgemont High uses two key locations relevant to teen lives and relationships — the mall and high school.

The family home serves as the central unifying locale in *The Royal Tenenbaums.*

Caddyshack centers its action on a gang of characters who hang out at Bushwood Country Club. Although *Caddyshack* blends an ensemble cast with sports comedy, the emphasis is more on the ensemble than sports. There are no training sequences, the stakes aren't particularly high, and the hero does not unify a team. The country club and its many ways of pitting the snobs versus the slobs is what brings everything together.

CHOOSING YOUR ENSEMBLE CHARACTERS

Ensemble characters can explore the central issue, or unifying force, from different perspectives. In this respect, we see the same world through different pairs of eyes. Your ensemble characters allow you to define various aspects of your unifying force.

For example, *Fast Times at Ridgemont High* deals with a group of teens finishing up the school year. The point of view of the story is seen through the eyes of the teens — the primary adults we see are the teachers. Part of their existence is spent in school, but an important aspect of their lives is centralized at the mall, where they work and relate. It's in this arena where our ensemble tries to live like adults, even though they're still teens. Each character represents a unique perspective in the work world, and the world of relationships.

Stacy (Jennifer Jason Leigh) wants to explore her sexuality and find a boyfriend. She has a successful job working at the mall's food court.

Her older brother, Brad (Judge Reinhold), wants a successful management job at the best burger place in town. He wants a commitment from his long-time girlfriend, but has a secret crush on Linda Barrett.

149

Mark "Rat" Ratner (Brian Backer) wants love and acceptance and is secretly in love with Stacy. He's an assistant to the assistant manager of the mall cinema, located on "the other side of the tracks" from the food court.

Mike Damone (Robert Romanus) is a concert ticket scalper and boastful womanizer who mentors "Rat."

Linda Barrett (Phoebe Cates) is also a mentor or confidant character who helps Stacy lose her virginity. She, like Damone, is quick to boast of her sexual experience (with her older college boyfriend).

Jeff Spicoli (Sean Penn) is a surfer dude who looks at the world with salt-water and pot-reddened eyes. He dreams of getting through school so he can enjoy life — riding the waves with a tasty buzz.

SURPRISE AND SUSPENSE IN ENSEMBLE

Surprise is definitely an integral part of the ensemble piece. With so many characters and distinct viewpoints, it is usually easier to generate surprise in an ensemble, more so than any other genre.

In *Parenthood*, many characters talk about the wisdom of their grand-mother, who's getting a little senile. When Gil's wife reminds him that he should listen to his Grandmother's advice, he snaps "If she's so smart, why is she sitting in our neighbor's car?" Sure enough, Grandma, ready to be driven back to the rest home, has gotten into the wrong car. This gives us an example of how a tiny, supporting character can be set up for a surprise laugh. We only know enough about Grandma to understand her comic perspective. She's the wise family elder. When the filmmakers twist that, we laugh.

Suspense is a key structural element used to help the storyteller effectively weave all of the subplots through the story. Suspense serves to make the audience wonder what will happen next. Will Rat and Stacy get together? Will Spicoli survive after ruining the football player's car? Will Brad dump his girlfriend?

A writer can use the suspense in one subplot to draw viewers into a new subplot. By ending a subplot at a suspenseful moment, specifically when a conflict resolution is in question, the writer can initiate or continue another storyline. Be careful that you don't drag the story down with too many subplots, or include a subplot that isn't very interesting. You don't want to get your audience angry because you've left them on a comic cliffhanger with one story and not provided them with an equally strong secondary or tertiary story.

CONNECTING THE DOTS

Using funny, connecting scenes can be the glue that holds your ensemble comedy together.

Hooks are useful in connecting scenes. For instance, *Fast Times* ends one scene with Spicoli wrecking Forest Whitaker's car. Spicoli's barely fazed, but the football player's worried little brother cries "First he's gonna shit, then he's gonna kill us." The next scene hooks us in by showing the damaged car covered by graffiti — allegedly from the football team's big rival. This gets Spicoli out of trouble and motivates the football player to kill his opponents during the big game.

Another technique is to leave causes dangling as you switch from one story to another. For example, in *Parenthood* we leave one scene with Todd brandishing a camera — wanting to record his love with Julie. Later we're linked back to this scene when we see Todd and Julie looking at pictures of Helen celebrating a promotion at work. They wonder what happened to their photos. Then we see Helen (Diane Weist) whimpering as she looks through photos of Julie and Todd naked. The scene plays even funnier because it has been set up so well.

151

EXERCISES:

1. Have we seen the special world of your ensemble comedy before?

2. How are you going to present this world so that it is unique and different?

3. What are the unique perspectives, viewpoints of your world? Can these be revealed by each of your ensemble characters?

4. Does one subplot stand out as your story's heart?

5. What device are you going to use to unify your ensemble cast (theme, locale, group, event)? Can your story support more than one?

6. Choose one of your favorite ensemble comedies. What are the unifying elements of the comedy?

7. Point out the dangling hooks between disparate storylines? Why do they succeed or fail?

A SELECTION OF SAMPLE ENSEMBLE COMEDIES FOR FURTHER STUDY:

Adventures of Priscilla, Queen of the Desert, The
American Graffiti
American Pie
Animal House
Caddyshack
Car Wash
Clerks
Dazed and Confused
Diner
Dogma
Fast Times at Ridgemont High
Gosford Park
Grand Hotel
Hannah and Her Sisters
M*A*S*H
Parenthood
Pulp Fiction
Pleasantville
Soapdish
Soul Food
Steel Magnolias

COMIC STRUCTURE 8 – FARCE

The **farce** relies more upon broad improbabilities of plot and characterization than clever wit. Characters are often selfish, having extreme, exaggerated points of view bordering on obsession. Memorable moments arise from farcical characters dealing with situations on the verge of chaos. Plots rely on absurd situations, slapstick, mistaken identities, outlandish deception, and surprising revelation.

Farces are an adult form of outrageous comedy, with characters serving their base needs, and situations commonly dealing with lust, sex, bodily fluids, and embarrassment.

SLAPSTICK ELEMENTS OF THE FARCE

Slapstick pits man against his environment. Objects and rooms take on a life of their own. Comedy stems from obstacles getting in the way of the character — a character rebounds off a wall, or door. But slapstick also plays with laughter fueling from incongruity — a character using an object in an illogical or unintended use. This is the comedy where a pie or bowl of oatmeal becomes a weapon. The character may need to dish out pain to another character but only by using objects in some unique way. A book becomes a bat, a two-by-four becomes a spring board.

In *There's Something About Mary*, Healy (Matt Dillon) knows he has to get past Magda's dog to win Mary's heart, so he drugs it. When Mary's in the kitchen, refilling drinks with Magda, Healy realizes that the dog has died and he has to bring it back to life. Healy tries giving doggie CPR, but that doesn't work, so he splices the wires from a table lamp and uses them as a defibrillator to shock the dog back to life. Then the dog catches fire and Healy dowses the flames with the water from a vase. When Mary and Magda appear from the kitchen, Mary tags the sequence with "What's that smell?"

Slapstick comedy can also be abuse comedy. What makes it work is the audience knows that the target of abuse is getting exactly what he deserves. A pie in the face is funnier if the victim is the pompous jerk we've hated for the last twenty minutes. Since everything is so outrageous in farce, we maintain comic distance and can laugh at the characters on screen — ha-ha it's happening to them and not us!

Slapstick can be the easiest form of comedy to write, and the most universal because of its visual nature. The comedy is executed from the elements on screen. And therefore the audience doesn't need to bring outside knowledge to sufficiently "get the joke." Chases, crashes, and food fights can quickly be set up and played out on screen. However, slapstick is difficult to sustain over the long haul. There's not much room to reveal character or motivation in a pie fight. Further, you run the risk of exhausting your audience.

CHARACTERS IN FARCE

Farcical characters will have needs that are easily understood — but exaggerated to the point of obsession. Even if the audience doesn't empathize with the characters, they understand the characters' selfish desires. In *There's Something About Mary*, everyone wants Mary. And Ted's motivation is beautifully set up. Mary is the perfect prom date. And she wants to go with him! But on his big night, Ted gets caught in his zipper and needs to be rushed to the hospital. In *The Producers*, Leo Bloom and Max Bialystock want to get rich, and they need an outlandish way to do it. In *A Fish Called Wanda*, the characters all want a piece of the diamond heist. All are base needs we can easily grasp.

The slapstick hero often holds a holier-than-thou or overly confident perspective of his skills. One technique to build your slapstick world is to simply put this hero into situations that collide with this inflated self-confidence. This comic perspective pushes the slapstick hero through obstacles, tests, and ordeals. Whatever may be dished out, the hero will never lose confidence. And as the situation deteriorates into

155

chaos, we laugh as the character attempts to prove he's still in control. A classic example of this slapstick hero is Inspector Clouseau in the Pink Panther movies. Jim Carrey, in *Ace Ventura* and *Dumb and Dumber*, continues this tradition of the slapstick hero who succeeds despite his incompetence.

THE MORE THE MERRIER

Farce is similar to ensemble comedy in that they both use a large cast of characters. It can be challenging to introduce these characters quickly and to make their appearances relevant to the special world. It can also be difficult to make these characters unique. Try to give each character a memorable perspective with a defined goal or motivation. A large cast of characters helps fuel the out-of-control nature of farce. Each character feels as if his story is the most important. Their selfish nature pits them as antagonists and shape shifters. This provides many layers of opposition for the hero, as well as subplots that threaten to derail, confuse, or complicate the main story.

FARCE'S OUTLANDISH DECEPTION

The selfish world of farce lends itself to deception. How far will a character go to get what they want? The cross-dressing comedies are the strongest visual examples (*Mrs. Doubtfire*, *Victor/Victoria*, *Tootsie*, and the classic *Some Like It Hot*). But deception doesn't necessitate putting on a physical disguise. The deception can be as simple as keeping one's obsession secret, or fabricating an outlandish plot to make money.

In *There's Something About Mary*, Ted hires a detective to find Mary. As the story plays out, a crazier deception is revealed: everyone is in love with Mary!

The Producers plan to create a sure-fire Broadway flop in order to keep the backers' money.

Comedy and suspense are built on how long the lie can keep going. Just like telling any lie, the deeper one gets into the deception, the stronger the inevitability of its revelation.

The commitment to the deception needs to be justified in the character's eyes. The stakes must be sufficient, and easily identifiable to the audience. In *Tootsie*, Michael Dorsey needs to take on the guise of Dorothy Michaels in order to get a job. He has no other choice.

A Fish Called Wanda is a farcical comedy of complications strung around a femme fatale hero, Wanda (Jamie Lee Curtis). All four of the male leads fall in love with Wanda and scheme to win her heart. (This plot device is paralleled in *There's Something About Mary*.) Wanda has no qualms about using her feminine wiles to get the $13 million in diamonds that the troupe has stolen.

The audience understands this goal and even though Wanda isn't particularly moral, the audience goes along with it because the stakes are high enough to warrant it — $13 million buys a lot of apologies.

For *The Producers*, it's money that drives Bloom and Bialystock. But on a deeper level, we discover that Leo Bloom has never taken a chance in life. Committing to the deception would grant Leo lessons in taking risks and living life.

There's Something About Mary relies heavily on compounding deception. Each of the four male leads (Ted, Woogie, Healy, and Tucker) all lie to Mary about their true motivations. This increases the stakes and raises suspense, as complications threaten to reveal Ted's initial deception of hiring the private investigator.

After Healy lays his eyes on Mary, he lies to Ted about what she looks like and then immediately quits his job and moves to Florida to win her heart. Healy listens in on Mary's conversations so he can become the exact kind of man she's looking for.

There can be so much deception in farce that even the audience gets confused. Occasionally, the characters may need to be brought together so the audience remembers why they are all going after the gold.

ALLIES IN FARCE

Allies are important for both the hero and the antagonist in farce. Since achieving the goal is usually difficult, if not impossible, two or more characters may form an alliance. However, when pressure is placed on this alliance the bonds will break. Allegiances in farce frequently snap in a comedic fashion, with the characters turning on each other just as quickly as they paired up. Anything goes, as long as it helps the characters pursue their goals. Allies in farce should not be trusted. They serve to compound the initial deception, and threaten to blow things up in your main character's face. Farce is like bad karma, what goes around comes around, and the deception will always be revealed.

THE COMEDY OF ERRORS

Part of the seductive nature of the farce's special world is that everything that can go wrong will. The audience is waiting for it. That is why they are salivating when the writer puts the hero in a situation that plays on both the character's worst fear and greatest desire. In farce, the worst thing that can happen does, and the opportunity to fulfill one's greatest wish will rear itself at the absolute worst moment.

In *A Fish Called Wanda*, Michael Palin plays Ken, a kind man with a stutter. We see that Ken is a devoted animal lover, and when his boss orders him to kill the old lady who is the only witness to their crime, we wonder how sweet, gentle Ken is going to do it. While trying to off the old lady, Ken accidentally kills all three of her dogs one by one. He is totally horrified by what he has done, he is almost a broken man. Luckily, the old lady finally drops dead of a heart attack. Ken accomplishes his mission, but the audience gets a good laugh at his pain and his worst fear — hurting animals!

158

Later, Ken suffers his worst nightmare. He is tormented by Otto (Kevin Kline) a psychopathic killer who reads philosophy. When Ken won't tell him where the loot is, Otto eats Ken's tropical fish — one by one — until Ken finally cracks.

THE SPECIAL WORLD IS ONE OF COINCIDENCE AND IMPLAUSIBILITY

The outrageous nature of farce can lead to a high level of coincidence and implausibility. These can be fun elements in farce. But they can be effectively "disguised" in order to keep the audience engaged in the story. Tools for "disguising" the story's coincidences and implausibility are 1.) sufficiently establishing character motivation, 2.) effectively planting and revealing set-ups and payoffs. What may seem implausible (everyone wants Mary), is logical in the special world of the farce. Yes, everyone really does want Mary!

Wanda justifies each implausible move she makes. She pretends to be in love with George, the lead bank robber. She plays Otto so that he'll go along with the heist, too, although the audience knows that she's not in love with him either, because she almost crowns him when he opens George's safe. When she sees the safe is empty, she realizes she needs Otto to help her find the loot. To get access to George in jail, Wanda poses as a legal student with a crush on George's barrister, Archie (John Cleese). Later, she even cures Ken's stutter with a heart-breaking kiss. Wanda mercilessly cons him out of revealing where the diamonds are.

Misunderstanding and coincidence run through farce like marbled veins of gold. However, the seeds of coincidence need to be planted discreetly and harvested when least expected. All coincidences should be set up in a way that is not obvious to the audience. For instance, Archie uses a co-worker's bachelor pad for an afternoon tryst with Wanda. He explains that the co-worker is on an assignment in Hong Kong and won't be back for months. Later, after Archie has stripped naked and seduced Wanda with Russian poetry, a family walks in on

159

him. They have just sublet the flat from the co-worker. Ironically, they know Archie — the same realtor sold Archie and his wife their house.

These brilliant bits show how heavily plotted the farce can be. They also underscore how important it is to use a red herring to throw the audience off course. In this case, Wanda's lust for hearing foreign languages has the audience laughing. John Cleese's funny striptease further distracts the audience so that they are genuinely surprised when the subletting family lets themselves into the flat.

Coincidence can add up to complications for both the hero and antagonists alike. When Otto breaks into Archie's house to warn him to stay away from Wanda, he is discovered by Archie's wife. He tells her that he is a CIA agent debriefing a suspect at a safe house nearby. Coincidentally, Fiona's father was in the English secret service. She knows that an agent would never tell a civilian that a debriefing was being held nearby.

THE ELIXIR IS A REVELATION

Inevitably the deception must be revealed. Indeed the "center cannot hold" as the character finds himself in a world that is crumbling from the weight of complications.

A key theme in a farce is confusion leading to freedom. In drama, we learn about our characters by the choices they make. In farce, once they commit to the deceptive special world, they lose their ability to make choices, and are swept down the rapids into a sea of chaos. The trials and tribulations that the character endures teaches them how to find their true self. That is the elixir of the farce. Confusion leads to chaos. Chaos leads to truth. Selfishness leads to self-sacrifice and celebration.

Amidst the complications and chaos with everyone proclaiming their love for Mary, Ted renounces his love. He has made the transformation from a meek character, too timid to pronounce his love, to one who does crazy things that aren't really him. He needed to renounce the love to become himself again. And he earns Mary's respect and love in the end.

At the end of *A Fish Called Wanda*, Archie chucks his boring and staid life for Wanda's uninhibited and unpredictable one. They fly to Rio to live happily ever after.

If the farce hero cannot see that this sacrifice must be made, they are doomed to repeat themselves.

At the end of *The Producers*, Bloom and Bialystock are rehearsing a new theatrical production in jail. The audience senses that there are many more scams to come from these two.

EXERCISES:

1. What are your characters' eccentricities? Are they sufficiently exaggerated to comic effect?

2. What is your character after? What is the outlandish deception that the hero creates to solve the problem?

3. How can you up the stakes, so that this special world becomes more plausible?

4. Does the audience need to identify with your farce hero? Why is your hero identifiable?

5. How can you make it more difficult for the farce hero?

6. How many other people in your story's world can be after the hero's goal?

7. Are there other forces that want to see the hero fail?

8. What is your hero's greatest wish? And what is his worst fear? Can these be important goals or obstacles in your story?

9. What about your special world lends itself to slapstick? What does your character hold dear that you will utterly and totally destroy?

A SELECTION OF FARCES FOR FURTHER STUDY:

Ace Ventura: Pet Detective
All of Me
Arsenic and Old Lace
Blame it on Rio
Drop Dead Fred
Groundhog Day
Liar Liar
Me, Myself & Irene
Mixed Nuts
Mouse Hunt
Rat Race
Skin Deep
Some Like It Hot
Spies Like Us
The Money Pit
The Producers
The Three Amigos
There's Something About Mary
Used Cars

COMIC STRUCTURE 9 – BLACK COMEDY

Black comedy uses humor as propaganda. It channels anger into a drive for societal change. One of the benefits of comedy is that it allows you to say hostile things with impunity. Humor points out the unfairness or stupidity inherent in the original, unacceptable situation.

We are going to look at three successful black comedies:

- *Citizen Ruth*
- *Heathers*
- *The War of the Roses*

TAKE AIM AT A SACRED COW

Good black comedy isn't always laugh-out-loud funny. It usually stings. Excellent black comedy leaves a mark. It points out how our society falsely worships a set of systems, institutions, or values. There is always a target in black comedy. For good results, black comedy needs an anti-establishment target. The bigger, the better (i.e., the military, the government, the educational system).

Citizen Ruth targets the abortion issue.

Heathers centers on teen suicide and the struggle to be popular.

The War of the Roses aims at divorce and its effects on a family.

In black comedy, the central conflict strives for institutional change. Something is wrong with the system and a Herculean effort is required to fix it. The situation may be unfixable and the hero will most likely fail, but that failure will bring enlightenment, either to those who have been left behind or to the viewer. The hero may not be aware that he is fighting or what he is fighting for. For instance, Ruth Stoops in *Citizen Ruth* is unaware that she has become a powerful symbol for each side of the abortion debate. She is only interested in who will pay her the most money. Regardless, the hero's ignorance will not be lost on the audience. The audience will learn a powerful lesson, even if the hero doesn't.

LOGIC LEADS TO RIDICULOUSNESS

Once the sacred cow is chosen, the writer can begin to build the black comedy by riffing on the potential absurdity of the story's situation. By exaggerating a story to its most ridiculous possible conclusion, black comedy reveals that the targeted system is absurd.

Black comedy explains the requirements of a particular system and then ridicules it. The results point out why these requirements or this system needs to change. *Citizen Ruth* explains the logic on both sides of the abortion debate and lets the viewer draw their own conclusion. *Heathers* explains what it takes to be popular and then shows us that it's not really important to be popular. *The War of the Roses* details what it takes to dissolve the state of holy matrimony and we learn that getting divorced often isn't worth it.

Black comedy imagines the failure of a system. Thus, we learn the value of black comedy: by saying something negative, the end result says something positive.

THE HERO'S GOAL IS OFTEN NEGATIVE

The hero's desire in a black comedy is typically negative. Ruth wants to get money to buy more drugs. Veronica wants to end the tyranny of popular high school students. Each of the Roses want to cause as much pain as possible for their soon-to-be ex-spouse. Heroes in black comedy often want to destroy or change a system that society holds dear. It is tough for the audience to root for someone who wants to take down a system, kill someone, or destroy an aspect of society — no matter how logical their motivation. Nonetheless, it is important for the lead character to provide a detailed explanation of their logic. The audience needs to understand the hero's motivation, even if they do not agree with the hero's logic. No matter how ridiculous the hero's motivation is, it will always contain a kernel of truth.

The hero of a black comedy may not be likable. Ruth Stoops (Laura Dern) in *Citizen Ruth* consistently makes the wrong choice. Veronica Sawyer (Winona Ryder) realizes that no matter how many Heathers she kills, someone will always rise to popularity and hold undeserved power over the student body. Barbara Rose (Kathleen Turner) takes a heartfelt note that her husband wrote to her on his "deathbed," thanking her for giving his life meaning, and uses it against him by turning it over to her divorce attorney.

Since the hero will be charismatic and passionate in crossing the threshold and justifying his or her motivation, the audience will accept their logic. No matter how many people around them tell them that they are crazy, the hero will stick to their convictions until the bitter end.

THE OPPONENT'S GOAL MAY ALSO BE NEGATIVE

An antagonist in a black comedy often wants the same goal as the hero, although for different reasons. The antagonist will also provide detailed justifications. They may be crazy — perhaps even crazier than the hero. We see this in *Citizen Ruth* when each side tries to one-up the other in order to get Ruth, a totally irredeemable character, to come to their side. J.D. (Christian Slater) in *Heathers* takes Veronica's wish to kill her friend literally. He serves as a dark mentor seducing her into the journey of bumping off the Heathers. This dovetails with Veronica's goal of making her high school nice, but by the end, he wants to orchestrate a mass teen suicide of the entire school. The spouses in *The War of the Roses* become equally zealous in their quest to destroy everything the other holds dear.

When the hero's goal is negative and the antagonist's goal is negative, we have a mathematical equation where two negatives make a positive. These two negatives show the audience just how ridiculous the entire situation is and the audience, almost against their will, illicitly roots for the success of the unsympathetic hero, who is the lesser of two evils.

AN ALLY WILL QUESTION THE HERO

The ally will tell the hero that what the hero is doing is absurd or crazy. The hero will not listen to the ally. This ally may be a mentor or articulate what the audience is thinking. This mentor serves as the voice of reason, but will most likely be ignored. For comedic sake, no one else in the story will listen to reason. There should be one character who recognizes the craziness ricocheting around a black comedy. In *Heathers*, Mrs. Fleming, the hippie teacher, tries to get the kids to talk about their feelings.

THE ORDEAL MAY DESTROY EVERYTHING

Black comedies build toward battles. The climatic battle will destroy the system that the hero has targeted. In these battles, people may be killed, or they may go crazy, and communities may be destroyed. In *Citizen Ruth*, each side of a movement is at stake. Despite these heightened stakes, the main characters will not learn anything from the ensuing devastation. In *Heathers*, J.D. has planted explosives to detonate during a school assembly. Veronica must endure an ordeal with J.D. and resurrect herself to save the school. In *The War of the Roses*, the ordeal does indeed destroy everything. Bit by bit, the Roses obliterate all of the possessions they value, reducing their house to rubble, and Oliver and Barbara are both killed. Once a kernel of motivation is planted, the stakes are escalated, leading to the destruction of the dark plan.

THE ELIXIR IN BLACK COMEDY IS WHAT THE CHARACTERS REFUSE TO LEARN

In certain black comedies, a narrator, or narrating device, lets us know what we've learned from the journey. This narrator can serve as a mentor to the audience.

Citizen Ruth does not use a narrator, however, Ruth often tells the audience exactly what she needs, whether it is drugs, alcohol, or money. Through each one of her horrible choices, Ruth exemplifies the worst example one can pick to base a moralistic movement on. Yet despite these shortcomings, each side of the issue champions Ruth like she is some noble creature worthy of a fight that would bring her case before the Supreme Court.

Gavin (Danny DeVito) in *The War of the Roses* tries to get his clients to listen to reason. The mentor fails and the Roses are killed, but their story scares another prospective divorce client so much that the character literally runs out of his attorney's office to keep his marriage together.

Heathers uses Veronica's diary to tell the audience what to learn from this journey. "Are we going to prom or hell?" Veronica furiously details the inanity of teen angst and questions the price of popularity. She writes that she wants to kill Heather. "Let me dream of a world without Heather. A world where I am free."

In another excellent black comedy, *The Opposite of Sex*, DeDee (Christina Ricci) serves as a sarcastic and cynical narrator. Her voiceover breaks in when we see a gun for the first time and says "This is called foreshadowing."

The use of a narrator can be a powerful mentor character or device. It can help you tell the audience exactly what they are supposed to learn from the perverted fairy tale that is black comedy.

Often the main characters in a black comedy do not get the final elixir. However, if the audience has paid attention, they reap the benefits. By withholding any sort of self-revelation from the main characters, the elixir or message is transferred directly to the audience. Occasionally, there is one sane character that has survived the devastation of the ordeal and they see a way out at the end of the film.

What do the characters in *Citizen Ruth* learn? Nothing, their hero's journey is a road to nowhere. They are still fighting in front of the abortion clinic as Ruth makes off with their money and disappears down the road to "huff" happily ever after. They do not realize that in their zeal to promote their cause, they have been duped by the most ignorant and immoral of foes. The antagonists are revealed as fools and the hero is not redeemed at the end. Does anyone learn anything from this ordeal? The reward is that the audience realizes that abortion is an individual, personal decision.

Veronica is redeemed at the end of *Heathers*. She chooses to kill her dark mentor, J.D., instead of allowing him to blow up the school. She learns that popularity is not worth killing for, or dying for.

In *The War of the Roses*, Barbara and Oliver destroy everything the other holds dear and then kill each other. They learn nothing from their journey. With her dying breath, Barbara pushes Oliver's hand off of her. She is totally without remorse. Even in death, she wants no part of their marriage. Though the characters have not been enlightened, the audience learns that material things aren't worth dying for and that often in divorce way too much time is spent fighting over tiny, insignificant issues.

EXERCISES:

1. What is the issue, institution, or sacred cow that you are skewering in your black comedy?

2. What is the logical extreme in your comic world?

3. At what point is your hero's world out of control?

4. Why does your hero want to change this institution? What is the hero targeting?

5. What is the antagonist's goal? How does it negatively impact the hero's goal?

6. What does the audience learn from the journey?

A SELECTION OF BLACK COMEDIES FOR FURTHER STUDY:

After Hours
Arsenic and Old Lace
Beetlejuice
Catch-22
A Clockwork Orange
The Cook, the Thief, His Wife and Her Lover
Delicatessen
Dr. Strangelove or: How I Learned to Stop Worrying and Love the Bomb
Eating Raoul
Fargo
Harold and Maude
Kind Hearts and Coronets
The Ladykillers
M*A*S*H
Monsieur Verdoux
Prizzi's Honor
Spanking the Monkey
Swimming with Sharks
Wild at Heart

COMIC STRUCTURE 10 –
SATIRE, PARODY & MOCKUMENTARY

This chapter explores three types of comedy, each defined by the target they are lampooning:

- satire: lampooning a social institution
- parody: lampooning a film genre
- mockumentary: lampooning the documentary

SATIRE

Satire uses derisive wit to expose the folly of mankind's social institutions. Satire criticizes through ridicule. Effective satire proves that the pen is indeed mightier than the sword, and denigrates institutions through scorn, irony, or exaggeration.

A satirist needs to have a critical attitude that points out what is wrong with the current system. The satirist's strong point of view, coupled with a deadly wit, will have the audience both laughing and wincing in pain.

GENERAL GUIDELINES

Satire goes hand-in-hand with black comedy because it is an aggressive form of comedy. Satire is usually angry and hostile. It delights in pointing out that something is rotten in Denmark. In this sense, satire echoes black comedy in that they both usually pick on a large, universal target. A satire will often attack an institution.

The ridiculousness of war is satirized in *M*A*S*H*. The machinations of the television business are satirized in *Network*. The dubious means and ends of politics are satirized in *Wag the Dog*. The medical profession is given a check-up in *Critical Care*. Even dead-end jobs and corporate ennui are satirized in *Office Space*, *Clerks*, and *Clockwatchers*.

These satires heap scorn and derision on the rules of the institution they are set in, in order to point out how ridiculous they are and how a return to the good old days is definitely in order.

AUDIENCE EXPECTATIONS

The audience expects a satire to challenge their beliefs. A satire will be smarter and more clever than most comedies. The writer will provide the audience with a reaffirmation of values. The work will show the desirability of maintaining society's standards and the necessity of reforming a corrupt system that has deviated from those standards.

BUILDING YOUR SATIRE

Effective techniques in satire can be ridicule, exaggeration, irony, comparison, and analogy. The main tool in the satirical arsenal is ridicule. The writer will also use devices of comparison and metaphor, which will show how the target of the satire is similar to something ludicrous.

Wag the Dog starts with the simple premise of a President willing to start a false war to mobilize public support and win re-election. The writers exaggerate the premise by adding accusations that the President was indiscreet with a "Firefly Girl." His handlers then hire a Hollywood producer to stage a fake war against Albania.

In *Wag the Dog*, a hired actress (Kirsten Dunst) runs across a soundstage while filmmakers digitally place her into a war-torn village. Computer enhancements change the terrified pet in her arms from a rabbit to a goat to a white kitten. This silly exercise shows the audience how easy it would be to "fake" a war and serves as a metaphor for the tightrope that spin doctors walk every day. When it is so easy to manipulate images to bend the truth, how quickly do things get out of control?

Effective satire causes the audience to examine their previously held beliefs. If you thought that political handlers were basically good, you might change your viewpoint by the end of *Wag the Dog*.

173

EXAGGERATION AND METAPHOR IN *NETWORK*

We can see the importance of exaggeration and metaphor as important tools for satire in *Network*. In *Network*, ratings go through the roof after Howard Beale threatens to kill himself on the air. The corporate bosses in charge of the network don't seem to care what goes on the air as long as it gets ratings. In fact, the network's programming executive, Diana Christensen (Faye Dunaway), champions a show about revolutionary urban-guerillas going on a crime spree.

As the plot progresses in *Network*, Diana slowly corrupts an accomplished news journalist Max Schumacher (William Holden). News blends with entertainment because news shows must solicit an audience, just like entertainment shows, as parent companies mandate that all programming must become profitable. The network news hour become "The Howard Beale Show" with a fortune-teller, gossip columnist, and a yellow journalist all sharing the stage with the mad prophet of the airwaves. The audience laughs because of the sheer, outrageous spectacle of it all.

The exaggeration in *Network* intensifies when Diana launches "The Mao Tse Tung Hour." The show is an instant hit. A hilarious scene follows as the communists become capitalists and abandon their revolutionary rhetoric and refuse to lower their distribution charges. This exaggeration reveals some irony in that even communists don't want to pay for overhead charges and production expenses.

The metaphors continue when Howard Beale's anti-Saudi rhetoric kills an important business deal with the Saudis. Beale is called onto the carpet by the owner of the network, Arthur Jensen (Ned Beatty). Jensen preaches through allegory that there is no America. There is no democracy. There is only IBM, ITT, and AT&T. DuPont, Dow, Union Carbide, and Exxon are the nations of the world today. Unfortunately, when Howard's monologues begin preaching of the demise of democracy, he alienates his audience and viewers desert him in droves.

174

HEROIC SACRIFICE

Whereas the hero in a black comedy often fails to learn a lesson from his journey, the hero in a satire is keenly aware of what they are doing and will make great sacrifices to achieve their goal.

In *Network*, Max knows he is repeating the pattern of the middle-aged executive when he starts his affair with Diana. They joke about the "script" of their affair.

In *Wag The Dog*, Stan Motss (Dustin Hoffman) is outraged when a senator ends his fake war in a speech. He's the producer, he'll decide when the war ends! This moment of conflict echoes the tail wagging the dog.

THE HERO RIDICULES AUTHORITY

As the satirist will use ridicule to skewer society, so too will the satire's hero. Hawkeye Pierce in *M*A*S*H* delights in exposing military clowns. He broadcasts Major Burns' and Hot Lips' tryst not just to be funny, but to expose the hypocrisy of the born-again and by-the-book characters of Burns and Houlihan.

Later Hawkeye demonstrates the hero's willingness to sacrifice — in this case his golf game — to defeat another military clown and give a Korean child a necessary operation.

THE JOURNEY TURNS OUT TO BE ONE OF IRONY

In *Network*, Howard Beale vows to kill himself on the air after he learns he is being fired. His ratings skyrocket and he becomes the mad prophet of the airwaves, only to be killed at the end of the film by revolutionary assassins. The film's narrator adds an ironic epitaph — this was the story of Howard Beale, the first known instance of a man who was killed because he had lousy ratings.

The audience has learned that nothing can be gained from blindly chasing ratings.

At the end of *M*A*S*H*, a great football game is won, but this is only a temporary diversion from a war that continues to maim and destroy.

EXERCISES:

1. What is wrong with the social institution you intend to satirize?

2. What kind of metaphors will your hero use to point out the flaws in the system?

3. In what ways can you exaggerate these flaws to ridicule the system?

4. Can subplots serve to underline your central thesis?

5. Is this world one that is universally understood? Will others agree with your point of view?

A SELECTION OF SATIRES FOR FURTHER STUDY:

Bananas
Being There
Bob Roberts
Bowfinger
Broadcast News
Bulworth
But I'm a Cheerleader
Dave
Dogma
EdTV
Election
Galaxy Quest
L.A. Story
Hollywood Shuffle
Still Crazy
The Muse
The Producers
The Truman Show
To Die For
The Player

PARODY

A parody spoofs a type of film or established film genre. Successful spoofs address a genre that is well-established in popular culture and the public eye. They have conventions and characters that are so ingrained as to become clichéd and stereotyped. Or the series has been so written to death, that it's begging for a comic homage.

Austin Powers is a parody of the 1960s spy films, including the James Bond franchise. *Airplane!* is a parody of the disaster movies that were popular in the 1970s. Recently, *Scary Movie*, *Scary Movie 2*, and *Not Another Teen Movie* all parodied the clichéd teen horror films of the 1990s.

GENERAL GUIDELINES

Although parody is an outrageous spin on a genre, it's an homage and nod of respect to a body of work. Best to parody a genre that you respect and love. You have to appreciate the genre you want to lampoon. Mel Brooks is a fan of westerns, and the classic Universal Frankenstein films. From this respect came his hilarious parodies *Blazing Saddles* and *Young Frankenstein*.

Like all comedy, parody isn't a string of gags and jokes. They need to come from a strong storyline and great characters. Woody Allen's early films (*Bananas*, *Sleeper*, *Take the Money and Run*, *Love and Death*) are wonderful parodies. The comic moments are structured around a stable, if not strong story line.

The spy movies of the 1960s were a big hit with audiences. In addition to the James Bond series, there was the Matt Helm series, the *Our Man Flint* series, the Harry Palmer spy series and *The Man from U.N.C.L.E.* *Austin Powers* delights in spoofing them all. Simple yet fairly solid story lines support the Austin Powers films. The story structure parodies the spy storyline, but, more important, the Austin Powers series mines the great hero/villain relationships that stand out in the best Bond thrillers.

Parody is serious. Even the outrageous *Airplane!* has a serious core to its story, Ted Striker's driving motivation is to regain his nerve to fly.

BUILDING YOUR PARODY

Choose a genre that is well-known, so well-known that the conventions can become clichés. Once you understand the conventions, start exploding them, riffing off of them or otherwise turning them on their ears.

The great moments in parody illustrate this technique. For instance, the campfire scene in *Blazing Saddles* shatters the myth of the western. The scene's scatological broaching of taboo destroys the romance of solitude on the prairie with a cacophony of flatulence. The scene uses truth, pain, exaggeration, and great pedestrian humor.

Jokes come fast and furious in parodies. However, realize that you may need to kill your best jokes if they don't fit the story. It is better to let your comic vision run wild in the first draft. You can always edit later. According to Mel Brooks, the first draft of *Blazing Saddles* came in at three-hundred plus pages. So, for the first draft, pile it all in. Feel free to riff on ideas.

RETHINKING CONVENTIONS

Mel Brooks is an expert at taking the cliché and spinning it in an unexpected way. In *Young Frankenstein*, there is a scene where Gene Wilder and Madeline Kahn are waiting on a train platform. They are the clichéd lovers that must part ways. Here, Brooks takes the opportunity to parody stylized romanticism. Madeline's character is more concerned about her taffeta dress, lipstick, hair, and nails than saying goodbye to her lover. After several awkward moments, the lovers resort to rubbing elbows as their "good-bye."

In *Blazing Saddles*, an evil posse charges up to a toll-booth in the middle of the desert. One character retorts "Someone's gotta go back and get a shit-load of dimes!"

Austin Powers rethinks conventions throughout its series. Dr. Evil and his son, Scott, argue about how to dispose of Austin Powers. Dr. Evil orders his crew to "Bring on the unnecessarily slow dipping mechanism." Scott tells his father he's got a gun in his room. "Let me go get it and I'll cap these guys."

This exchange is obviously a knowing wink at the outlandish predicaments that James Bond always escapes from. However, Scott and Dr. Evil argue their own points in earnest and reveal another layer of comedy. In a series of running gags, the audience learns that these characters are trying to rebuild their fractured relationship. In an earlier bit, Scott and Dr. Evil try group therapy. In the sequel, they go on *The Jerry Springer Show* to talk about their relationship troubles.

This bit also demonstrates the art of riffing, a technique in building lampoons. *Austin Powers* looks at the modern convention of pop psychology and makes it funnier by tailoring it for a psychotic killer, bent on world domination, and his son, who can't get along. The comedy comes from seeing this convention from another perspective. These two unlikely characters want to make their relationship stronger — even though they are also trying to destroy the world.

COMIC TECHNIQUES IN PARODY

The most common comic techniques are probably understatement, homage, literalness, repetition, exaggeration, and wordplay.

Austin Powers uses understatement when Dr. Evil asks the United Nations for one million dollars.

One of the best jokes in the movie *Airplane!* comes in the form of an homage to *From Here to Eternity*. Robert Hays and Julie Hagerty kiss on the beach. They roll romantically on the sand in the throes of passion as the ocean gently laps at their feet. Suddenly, a huge wave pounds them, sending bushels of seaweed and ocean trash over the lovers.

Airplane! is also filled with eccentric characters, most all of whom take every word seriously, if not literally.

                    DOCTOR
         Tell the Captain we've got
         to land as soon as we can.
         This woman has to be gotten
         to a hospital.

                    STEWARDESS
         A hospital? What is it?

                    DOCTOR
         It's a big building with
         patients, but that's
         not important right now.

Later an old lady notices that the hero, Ted Striker (Robert Hays) is apprehensive about the plane taking off.

                    OLD LADY
         Nervous?

                    TED
         Yes.

                    OLD LADY
         First time?

                    TED
          No, I've been nervous
          lots of times.

This literalness becomes a running gag throughout the film.

The filmmakers even milk comedy out of the pilots' names. Anything
that generates confusion can get a laugh.

                    ROGER MURDOCK
          We have clearance, Clarence.

                    CAPTAIN OVEUR
          Roger, Roger. What's
          our vector, Victor?

                    TOWER VOICE
          Tower's radio clearance, over!

                    CAPTAIN OVEUR
          That's Clarence Oveur! Oveur.

                    TOWER VOICE
          Roger.

                    ROGER MURDOCK
          Huh?

                    TOWER VOICE
          Roger, over.

                    ROGER MURDOCK
          Huh?

                    CAPTAIN OVEUR
          Huh?

                    182

This madcap, anything goes riffing is a key element in parody, because the audience won't mind if you wander off point for a while as long as you are funny and return to the story when the laughs die down.

Parody can become a tricky business because you have to accurately gauge how much your audience knows about your target. The target of your metaphorical pie-in-the-face is often someone or something outside the story.

The best parody operates on two levels at the same time. You might have a fish-out-of-water tale that involves a comic character in a new and challenging world and yet, at the same time, mocks a facet of the world with which we're quite familiar. If you stray too far from "reality," you run the risk that the audience might not bother to return to your special world. This re-emphasizes the need for a strong, compelling story to bring the audience back if a joke takes them off the page.

CHARACTER COMMITMENT

We mentioned earlier that parody is serious business. You must develop a strong story foundation which includes character development. Parody requires total character commitment coupled with strong needs and goals. The actor will fail if they play the moment for the laughs. They must play the seriousness of the situation and let the audience see the comedy. And the parody writer must provide this serious character foundation from which the best parody succeeds: strong character goals, identifiable needs and desires, and solid convictions. In most cases, the comedy will fail if the character comes across as if he is "in" on the joke.

EXERCISES:

1. Identify five conventions from the genre you want to parody.

2. What are the clichés in the genre you want to parody?

3. How can you twist these clichés and conventions so they reveal another story?

4. Does your parody's storyline have a strong structure to support your gags? Are your characters acting with strong goals and convictions to engage your audience?

A SELECTION OF PARODIES FOR FURTHER STUDY:

Airplane!
Austin Powers: Goldmember
Austin Powers: International Man of Mystery
Austin Powers: The Spy Who Shagged Me
Blazing Saddles
Hot Shots!
Hot Shots! Part Duex
Jane Austen's Mafia
Kentucky Fried Movie
Police Academy
Scary Movie
Scary Movie 2
Shanghai Noon
Spy Hard
Stiff Upper Lips
The Naked Gun: From the Files of Police Squad!
Top Secret
Wrongfully Accused

MOCKUMENTARY

A mockumentary is an intentional parody or "mocking" of the documentary format. Mockumentary's homage can include focusing on limited comic arenas, incorporating documentary techniques, and using the documentary filming process in an attempt to catch "real life" on screen. Mockmentaries often rely on improvisation by an ensemble of comic actors to achieve this honest view of a subculture in society. Of course, it's still a comedy, but mockumentaries succeed when characters and situation are rooted firmly in seriousness. The audience may even question: this is a comedy, right? Or is this for real?

The mockumentary itself acts as a straight-man, and makes the ridiculous or obscure subject being filmed even funnier by suggesting that the audience take a serious look at it.

GENERAL GUIDELINES

Mockumentaries are often set in limited comic arenas. *This Is Spinal Tap* parodies the rock documentary. *Waiting for Guffman* is about a community theatre production with aspirations of making it big. *Best in Show* is about obsessive dog show participants. These limited comic arenas take advantage of the primary purpose of documentaries — to inform people about a unique and special world.

The style of the film offers lots of room to educate the audience about the special world. The audience anticipates that documentaries will have some level of teaching. However, mockumentaries are crafted with identifiable desires. Their heroes want fame, victory, and self-worth. These goals help the audience identify with the characters, when their world may otherwise be obscure or distant.

The mockumentary lampoons the documentary style and process and, out of necessity, incorporates, and riffs off of this film style's techniques. These include using an authoritative narrator, "real" footage of the event, historical photographs, archival documents, fly-on-the-wall footage, and interviews with experts or eyewitnesses.

COMIC TECHNIQUES IN MOCKUMENTARY

Conviction and exaggeration are key elements in mockumentaries. The documentary often deals with ordinary people being interviewed, but they offer a unique perspective of life — the subject of the documentary. They are not in on the joke. To them, this is deadly serious.

Running gags are also popular bridges in mockumentaries. *This Is Spinal Tap* kills off 37 drummers in spectacular fashion, one chokes on someone else's vomit, and another spontaneously combusts. *Best in Show* keeps having ex-lovers of Cookie (Catherine O'Hara) pop out of the woodwork, keeping her husband (Eugene Levy) in a perpetual state of sheepish embarrassment. Running gags serve to unify a meandering storyline and snap the viewer back into the proper context of the mockumentary.

Marty DiBergi (Rob Reiner) trains his cameras on the members of Spinal Tap as they tell him how they began their careers as The Originals, but there was already a band called The Originals, so then they changed their name to The New Originals and later became Spinal Tap. After all, "It's such a fine line between stupid and clever," says guitarist David St. Hubbins (Michael McKean). Ignorant understatements like this run throughout the film.

The members of Spinal Tap are exaggerated caricatures of heavy metal musicians. The band's bass player, played by Harry Shearer, is appropriately named Derek Smalls. He is later stopped at the airport when the cucumber wrapped in aluminum foil in his pants sets off a security alarm.

During the film, we see clips of the band during early appearances on English television. These are comical homages to early Beatles appearances on *Top of the Pops*.

Later the band is victimized by literalness when the Stonehenge props they drew on a bar napkin show up as miniatures only eighteen inches tall.

As the members of Spinal Tap encounter obstacles on the road, director Marty DeBergi asks them how they are feeling. "I'd feel much worse if I weren't under heavy medication," retorts guitarist David St. Hubbins.

Best in Show revolves around obsessive and dysfunctional contestants competing in the Mayflower Dog Show. The mockumentary concentrates on five participants competing in the show. The filmmakers create layers of conflict through each scene from seemingly innocent things, barely related to the story — a busy bee chew toy, past lovers, and even a knee injury.

NARRATOR AS BOTH MENTOR AND HERO

This Is Spinal Tap is narrated by Marty DiBergi (Rob Reiner). He's a bad director seriously trying to document an English heavy metal band's first tour in six years. Although he is inept, it is clear he is a legitimate fan of the band, and serves as a mentor or authority figure for the audience. His narration at the beginning of the film tells us so.

Other mockumentaries use an anonymous voice-over narration that mimics the sound of an actual documentary (*Zelig, Take the Money and Run*). Again, this serves to guide the audience, as well as effectively set the film's style.

Best in Show uses commentators Buck Laughlin (Fred Willard) and Trevor Beckwith (Jim Piddock) to provide additional insight and silliness into the world of the dog show. Buck is a trickster or clown with Beckwith his aggrieved straight man.

ALLIES AND EXPERTS

Fly-on-the-wall footage can provide the viewers of a mockumentary with varying perspectives. We see each hero team preparing for the Mayflower Dog Show and learn how serious the competition is in this cutthroat arena.

So-called experts enlighten the audience as to what our character's role really is in the special world of the mockumentary. When these characters are interviewed, they will place things in context. These contexts will show the audience whether the characters in the mockumentary are succeeding or failing. Frequently, the audience sees both the failings and the successes of the characters, which will provide better empathy.

PURPOSE OF THE MOCKUMENTARY

Mockumentaries demonstrate how easy it is to fake codes and conventions, and can ultimately force us to consider the nature of the documentary itself. Why do we give so much importance to it? Just because someone bothered to light a subject and film it, is it really worthy of our time? Mockumentaries offer a unique arena for laughter and entertainment while making us question — why are we doing this with our time? Upon reflection, a mockumentary viewer may realize that good filmmakers can make even the silliest of viewpoints seem reasonable.

EXERCISES:

1. What subculture or social issue can you deconstruct for your mockumentary?

2. What perspectives of this world are represented by your ensemble of characters? In what ways can the audience identify with your characters?

3. What elements of mockumentary do reality shows like *The Jamie Kennedy Experiment* and *The Tom Green Show* usurp?

4. How much does your audience know about the comic arena of your mockumentary? What documentary techniques can visually and comically facilitate any necessary exposition?

5. Does a filmmaker have the responsibility to announce — this is a mockumentary? What is the difference between a mockumentary and a hoax?

A SELECTION OF MOCKUMENTARIES FOR FURTHER
STUDY:

A Hard Day's Night
Bananas
Best in Show
Fear of a Black Hat
Superguy: Behind The Cape
Take the Money and Run
Teddy Bear's Picnic
This Is Spinal Tap
Waiting for Guffman
Zelig

CONCLUSION
THE END OF THE LAUGHTER?

Thank you for taking this journey of comic genre analysis. Each comic genre has its own set of story patterns, unique heroes, opponents, obstacles, and themes. It is important to know the expectations of each genre. Some writers look down on genre writing, believing it to be formulaic and weak. They think that genre serves only as a blueprint for clichéd storytelling. However, knowing these forms gives you the ability to transcend them, and delight the audience with originality and surprise.

The intent of this text is to alert the reader to the steps that are necessary to meet audience expectations for a particular genre. We do not want you to repeat worn clichés by merely retracing steps we've seen a million times. Rather, now that you know the rules, start to break them. Since you know that the audience is expecting something, subvert their expectations and surprise them. They'll love you all the more for it.

So think of genre as a strategy for storytelling. Genre establishes a framework for your hero's journey. Is your central question one that would be best answered by a military trickster or a frustrated and lonely teenager? Knowing how the various genres impart their lessons and themes may make storytelling easier.

Compiling this book has been challenging in that what provides insight for one reader is stating the obvious for another. Many of you will not agree with some of the analysis and examples we've included. Drawing your own interpretations is what storytelling is for. Story brings meaning to our lives. Obviously some stories resonate more with people who have had similar experiences. If you begin to hold these perspectives we've presented here to your own significant comedies, and if these techniques offer ways to appreciate a comedy's success or understand a comedy's failings, then we feel we have fulfilled our quest.

Comedy is often given second-class genre status as pure entertainment, yet comedy allows us to see ourselves and our world in a powerful light. We can celebrate our most cherished gifts, and destroy our most threatening fears, with the elixir of laughter. Perhaps comedy's greatest power is to mock what we don't understand. Through comedy we can subvert what is out of our control. No matter how bad things get in our lives, if we can poke fun at others and ourselves, somehow things aren't so bad. Sometimes laughter really is the best medicine.

Respect the power of the written word by being the best writer you can be. Now that you've finished reading this book, get back to your keyboard and write something that will make us laugh.

APPENDIX A:
THE STAGES OF THE HERO'S JOURNEY

(reprinted from *Myth and the Movies*, by Stuart Voytilla)

All stories consist of common structural elements or stages found universally in myths, fairy tales, dreams, and movies. These twelve stages compose the hero's journey. What follows is a simple overview of each stage, illustrating basic characteristics and functions. Use it as a quick reference guide as you explore the genre and movie analyses. Since it cannot provide all of Christopher Vogler's insights upon which it was based, I recommend you refer to his book, *The Writer's Journey*, for a much more thorough evaluation of these stages.

The paradigm that follows illustrates the "traditional" hero's journey as seen in the majority of stories. As you explore the film and genre analyses that follow you'll find that the hero's journey provides a flexible and adaptable model with the potential for an infinite variety of shapes and progressions of stages. The journey's stages may be avoided, or repeated, or shifted about depending upon the needs of the individual story.

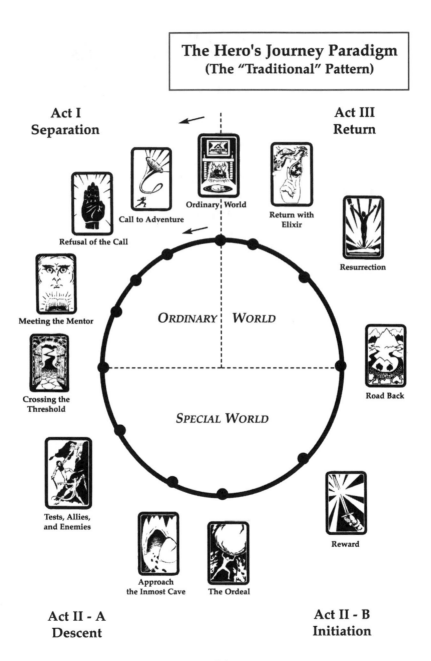

The Hero's Journey Paradigm
(The "Traditional" Pattern)

Act I
Separation

Act III
Return

Ordinary World

Call to Adventure

Refusal of the Call

Return with
Elixir

Meeting the Mentor

Resurrection

ORDINARY WORLD

Crossing the
Threshold

Road Back

SPECIAL WORLD

Tests, Allies,
and Enemies

Approach
the Inmost Cave

The Ordeal

Reward

Act II - A
Descent

Act II - B
Initiation

Ordinary World

The Audience meets the Hero in the **Ordinary World**.

Call to Adventure

The Hero receives the **Call to Adventure**, a challenge, a quest, or a problem that must be faced.

Refusal of the Call

The Hero expresses fear and is Reluctant or **Refuses the Call**.

Meeting the Mentor

A **Meeting with the Mentor** provides encouragement, wisdom or magical gifts to push the Hero past fear and doubt.

Crossing the Threshold

The Hero finally accepts the challenge and **Crosses the Threshold** into the Special World.

Tests, Allies, and Enemies

The Hero learns about the Special World through **Tests**, encountering **Allies and Enemies**.

Approach the Inmost Cave

The Hero makes the final preparations and **Approaches the Inmost Cave**.

Ordeal

The Hero endures the **Ordeal**, the central crisis in which the Hero confronts his greatest fear and tastes death.

Reward

The Hero enjoys the **Reward** of having confronted fear and death.

Road Back

The Hero takes the **Road Back** and recommits to completing the Journey.

Resurrection

The Hero faces the climactic ordeal, **Resurrection**, that purifies, redeems, and transforms the Hero on the Threshold home.

Return with Elixir

The Hero **Returns with the Elixir** to benefit the Ordinary World.

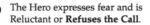
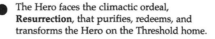

THE CHARACTER ARC

The symbolism of the journey's stages ("Crossing the Threshold," "Approach the Inmost Cave," "Return with the Elixir") can easily mislead us into seeing the paradigm as representing a purely physical journey. Indeed the hero takes a physical, active part on the journey to solve a problem or achieve a goal. But the hero's journey is as important an emotional or psychological journey as it is physical. A character's actions and decisions in response to the journey's stages can reveal the character arc, or phases of growth that a character makes during the course of the story. The following illustrates the character arc using the icons representing the journey's stages for reference.

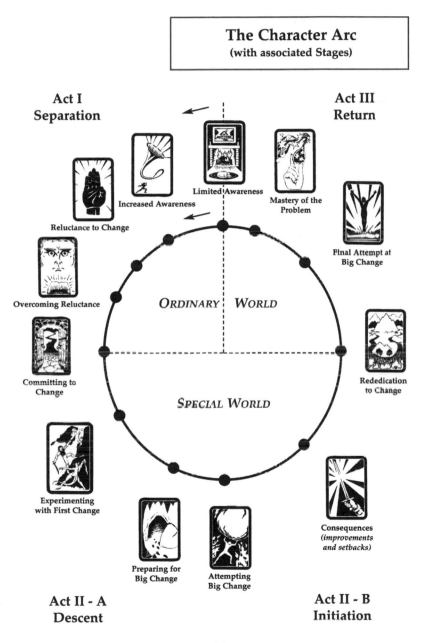

The Character Arc
(with associated Stages)

Act I
Separation

Act III
Return

Limited Awareness

Increased Awareness

Mastery of the
Problem

Reluctance to Change

Final Attempt at
Big Change

Overcoming Reluctance

ORDINARY WORLD

Committing to
Change

Rededication
to Change

SPECIAL WORLD

Experimenting
with First Change

Consequences
(*improvements
and setbacks*)

Preparing for
Big Change

Attempting
Big Change

Act II - A
Descent

Act II - B
Initiation

THE ORDINARY WORLD

The ordinary world allows us to get to know the hero and identify with him before the journey begins. Since the audience usually experiences the journey through the hero's eyes, we must be able to relate to him. The ordinary world gives us the opportunity to identify with the hero's drives, urges, and problems, while showing unique characteristics and flaws that make him three-dimensional. The hero's inner and outer problems may be established, although these can change depending upon the demands of the journey. Shrek's problems in his ordinary world (to reclaim his swamp and solitude) change drastically when he enters the special world, as heroic retriever of Princess Fiona.

Every story involves a problem or central dramatic question that disrupts the ordinary world. The hero must enter the special world to solve the problem, answer the dramatic question, and return balance. The ordinary world allows the storyteller to contrast the ordinary and special worlds. The ordinary world is the hero's home, the safe haven upon which the special world and the journey's outcome must be compared. Areas of contrast can include the special world's physical and emotional characteristics, its rules and inhabitants, as well as the hero's actions and growth while traveling through this special world.

THE CALL TO ADVENTURE

The call to adventure sets the story rolling by disrupting the comfort of the hero's ordinary world, presenting a challenge or quest that must be undertaken. The call sets the ordinary world off balance, and establishes the stakes involved if the challenge is rejected. Often delivered by the herald archetype, the call to adventure can take a multitude of forms including: a message or announcement, a sudden storm, the arrival of the villain, a death, an abduction, a man's dying words.

The hero may need a succession of calls before finally realizing that a challenge must be met, or that his only means of escape is the special world. Many times the hero needs to choose between two conflicting calls.

REFUSAL OF THE CALL

A hero refuses the journey because of fears and insecurities that have surfaced from the call to adventure. The hero is not willing to make changes, preferring the safe haven of the ordinary world.

The refusal of the call becomes an essential stage that communicates the risks involved in the journey that lies ahead. Without risks and danger or the likelihood of failure, the audience will not be compelled to be a part of the hero's journey.

Although an eager or willing hero may skip the refusal stage, the hero's allies or threshold guardians may still express the fears and risks involved.

In horror and thriller, the frightening and forbidding nature of the special world can lead the hero to being repeatedly "called" to the adventure that he continues to refuse. Each call and refusal must escalate the stakes until the hero has no choice but to accept the call.

MEETING THE MENTOR

The hero meets a mentor to gain confidence, insight, advice, training, or magical gifts to overcome the initial fears and face the threshold of the adventure.

A hero may not wish to rush into a special world blindly and seeks the experiences and wisdom of someone who has been there before. This mentor has survived to provide the essential lessons and training needed to better face the journey's tests and ordeals. The mentor may be a physical person, or an object such as a map, a logbook, or hieroglyphics. In westerns and detective stories, the hero may hold an inner mentor, a strong code of honor or justice that guides him through the journey.

CROSSING THE THRESHOLD

Crossing the threshold signifies that the hero has finally committed to the journey. He is prepared to cross the gateway that separates the ordinary world from the special world. The crossing may need more than accepting one's fears, a map, or a swift kick in the rear from a mentor. The hero must confront an event that forces him to commit to entering the special world from which there is no turning back.

The event will re-establish the central dramatic question that propels the story forward. The event will directly affect the hero, raising the stakes and forcing some action.

Outside forces may push the hero ahead, such as an abduction of someone close to the hero. A chase may push the hero to the brink presenting no choice but to commit. The hero's place in his ordinary world may be usurped by the villain or rival, or the hero crosses the threshold with guns blazing and whip cracking.

Internal forces may also push the hero to accept his special world. Alvy and Annie agree to share that first kiss of commitment (*Annie Hall*).

TESTS, ALLIES, ENEMIES

Having crossed the threshold, the hero faces tests, encounters allies, confronts enemies, and learns the rules of this special world. This stage is important for hero and audience alike. Whether entering the imaginary world of a future society or the emotional realms of romantic love, the test stage is our first look at the special world and how its conditions and inhabitants contrast with the hero's ordinary world.

The hero needs to find out who can be trusted. Allies are earned, a side-kick may join up, or an entire hero team forged. Enemies and villains are encountered. A rival to the hero's goal may reveal himself.

The hero must prepare himself for the greater ordeals yet to come and needs this stage to test his skills and powers, or perhaps seek further training from the mentor. This initiation into the special world also tests the hero's commitment to the journey, and questions whether he can succeed.

APPROACH TO THE INMOST CAVE

The hero must make the preparations needed to approach the inmost cave that leads to the journey's heart, or central ordeal. Maps may be reviewed, attacks planned, a reconnaissance launched, and possibly the enemy's forces whittled down, before the hero can face his greatest fear or the supreme danger lurking in the special world. The confident hero may bypass these preparations and make a bold approach to the inmost cave.

The hero has survived his descent into the special world. He has earned his place and may need to take a break for a cigarette and a joke, or a romance, before forging to the ordeal. A hero's team may have hit setbacks during the tests, and the approach is necessary to reorganize the depleted ranks, remember the dead and wounded, and rekindle morale with a hero's or mentor's rally cry.

The approach can signal a ticking clock or a heightening of the stakes. In romantic comedy, the approach can force the lovers to question commitment; one partner may express the need for marriage.

THE ORDEAL

The hero engages in the ordeal, the central life-or-death crisis, during which he faces his greatest fear, confronts his hardest challenge, and experiences "death." His journey teeters on the brink of failure. And the audience watches in suspense wondering whether the hero will survive. The ordeal is the central, essential, and magical stage of any journey. Only through "death" can the hero be reborn, experiencing a resurrection that grants greater powers or insight to see the journey to the end.

The hero may directly taste death, or witness the death of an ally or mentor, or even worse directly cause that death. The ordeal may pit hero against shadow or villain, and the hero's failure heightens the stakes and questions the journey's success. The hero may have the powers to defeat a villain in the ordeal, only to have to face greater forces in the journey's second half.

In romantic comedies, death can mean the break-up of the relationship. In romance, a crisis of the heart can be a love scene — the physical act of love is a type of "death" or surrender. The crisis of the heart can also be a moment when a shapeshifting lover suddenly reveals a dark side that attempts to destroy the hero.

REWARD

The hero has survived death, overcome his greatest fear, slain the dragon, or weathered the crisis of the heart, and now earns the reward that they sought. The hero's reward comes in many forms: a magical sword, an elixir, greater knowledge or insight, reconciliation with a lover. Whatever the treasure, the hero has earned the right to celebrate. Celebration not only allows the hero to replenish his energy, but also gives the audience a moment to catch their breath before the journey resumes to its climax and resolution.

The hero may have earned the reward outright, or the hero may have seen no option but to steal it. The hero may rationalize this elixir theft having paid for it with the tests and ordeals thus far. But the consequences of the theft must be confronted as the shadow forces race to reclaim the elixir that must not see the light of the ordinary world.

THE ROAD BACK

The hero must finally recommit to completing the journey and accept the road back to the ordinary world. A hero's success in the special world may make it difficult to return. Like crossing the threshold, the road back, needs an event that will push the hero through the threshold, back into the ordinary world.

The event should re-establish the central dramatic question, pushing the hero to action and heightening the stakes. Like any strong turning point, the action initiating the road back could change the direction of the story. The hero may need a force to chase him out of the special world. A ticking clock threatening destruction or death in the ordinary world may be set in motion. The villain may have recovered the elixir and must be stopped.

The event may be an internal decision that must be made by the hero. In comedies, a hero may be trying to juggle conflicting journeys, and one must finally be sacrificed. In romance and action adventure, the road back may be a moment when the hero must choose between the journey of a higher cause versus the personal journey of the heart.

THE RESURRECTION

The hero faces the resurrection, his most dangerous meeting with death. This final life-and-death ordeal shows that the hero has maintained and can apply all that he has brought back to the ordinary world.

This ordeal and resurrection can represent a "cleansing" or purification that must occur now that the hero has emerged from the land of the dead. The hero is reborn or transformed with the attributes of his ordinary self in addition to the lessons and insights from the characters that he has met along the road.

The resurrection may be a physical ordeal, or final showdown between hero and shadow; however, the ticking clock of the road back has been set. This battle is for much more than the hero's life. Other lives, or an entire world may be at stake and the hero must now prove that he has achieved heroic status and willingly accept his sacrifice for the benefit of the ordinary world.

Other allies may come to the last minute rescue to lend assistance, but in the end the hero must rise to the sacrifice at hand. He must deliver the blow that destroys the villain's plan, or offer his hand and accept the "magic" elixir of love.

RETURN WITH THE ELIXIR

The return with the elixir is the final reward earned on the hero's journey. The hero has been resurrected, purified and earned the right to be accepted back into the ordinary world and share the elixir of the journey. The true hero returns with an elixir to share with others or heal a wounded land. The elixir can be a great treasure or magic potion. It could be love, wisdom, or simply the experience of surviving the special world. Even the tragic end of a hero's journey can yield the best elixir of all, granting the audience greater awareness of us and our world. The hero may show the benefit of the elixir, using it to heal a physical or emotional wound, or accomplishing tasks that had been feared in the ordinary world. The return signals a time when we distribute rewards and punishments, or celebrate the journey's end with revelry or marriage.

The elixir may bring closure to the journey and restore balance to the ordinary world. Possibly it poses questions and ambiguities that continues the journey beyond the final "fade out."

In most tales, the return with the elixir completes the cycle of this particular journey. Story lines have been resolved, balance has been restored to the ordinary world, and the hero may now embark on a new life, forever influenced by the journey traveled.

APPENDIX B:
AFI'S 100 YEARS... 100 LAUGHS

1	*SOME LIKE IT HOT*	1959
2	*TOOTSIE*	1982
3	*DR. STRANGELOVE OR: HOW I LEARNED TO STOP WORRYING AND LOVE THE BOMB*	1964
4	*ANNIE HALL*	1977
5	*DUCK SOUP*	1933
6	*BLAZING SADDLES*	1974
7	*M*A*S*H*	1970
8	*IT HAPPENED ONE NIGHT*	1934
9	*THE GRADUATE*	1967
10	*AIRPLANE!*	1980
11	*THE PRODUCERS*	1968
12	*A NIGHT AT THE OPERA*	1935
13	*YOUNG FRANKENSTEIN*	1974
14	*BRINGING UP BABY*	1938
15	*THE PHILADELPHIA STORY*	1940
16	*SINGIN' IN THE RAIN*	1952
17	*THE ODD COUPLE*	1968
18	*THE GENERAL*	1927
19	*HIS GIRL FRIDAY*	1940
20	*THE APARTMENT*	1960

21	*A FISH CALLED WANDA*	1988
22	*ADAM'S RIB*	1949
23	*WHEN HARRY MET SALLY…*	1989
24	*BORN YESTERDAY*	1950
25	*THE GOLD RUSH*	1925
26	*BEING THERE*	1979
27	*THERE'S SOMETHING ABOUT MARY*	1998
28	*GHOSTBUSTERS*	1984
29	*THIS IS SPINAL TAP*	1984
30	*ARSENIC AND OLD LACE*	1944
31	*RAISING ARIZONA*	1987
32	*THE THIN MAN*	1934
33	*MODERN TIMES*	1936
34	*GROUNDHOG DAY*	1993
35	*HARVEY*	1950
36	*NATIONAL LAMPOON'S ANIMAL HOUSE*	1978
37	*THE GREAT DICTATOR*	1940
38	*CITY LIGHTS*	1931
39	*SULLIVAN'S TRAVELS*	1941
40	*IT'S A MAD, MAD, MAD, MAD WORLD*	1963
41	*MOONSTRUCK*	1987
42	*BIG*	1988
43	*AMERICAN GRAFFITI*	1973

67	*MRS. DOUBTFIRE*	1993
68	*THE AWFUL TRUTH*	1937
69	*BANANAS*	1971
70	*MR. DEEDS GOES TO TOWN*	1936
71	*CADDYSHACK*	1980
72	*MR. BLANDINGS BUILDS HIS DREAM HOUSE*	1948
73	*MONKEY BUSINESS*	1931
74	*9 TO 5*	1980
75	*SHE DONE HIM WRONG*	1933
76	*VICTOR/VICTORIA*	1982
77	*THE PALM BEACH STORY*	1942
78	*ROAD TO MOROCCO*	1942
79	*THE FRESHMAN*	1925
80	*SLEEPER*	1973
81	*THE NAVIGATOR*	1924
82	*PRIVATE BENJAMIN*	1980
83	*FATHER OF THE BRIDE*	1950
84	*LOST IN AMERICA*	1985
85	*DINNER AT EIGHT*	1933
86	*CITY SLICKERS*	1991
87	*FAST TIMES AT RIDGEMONT HIGH*	1982
88	*BEETLEJUICE*	1988
89	*THE JERK*	1979

90	*WOMAN OF THE YEAR*	1942
91	*THE HEARTBREAK KID*	1972
92	*BALL OF FIRE*	1941
93	*FARGO*	1996
94	*AUNTIE MAME*	1958
95	*SILVER STREAK*	1976
96	*SONS OF THE DESERT*	1933
97	*BULL DURHAM*	1988
98	*THE COURT JESTER*	1956
99	*THE NUTTY PROFESSOR*	1963
100	*GOOD MORNING, VIETNAM*	1987

APPENDIX C:
TOP TEN COMEDIES FROM THE LAST FIVE YEARS

Top 10 Comedies of 1997	US BO (in $mil)	Studio
Men in Black	$250.20	Sony
Liar Liar	$181.40	Universal
As Good As It Gets	$130.00	Sony
My Best Friend's Wedding	$126.80	Sony
George of the Jungle	$105.20	Disney
Flubber	$95.00	Disney
In & Out	$63.80	Paramount
Mouse Hunt	$60.00	DreamWorks
Jungle 2 Jungle	$59.90	Disney
Austin Powers	$53.80	New Line

Top 10 Comedies of 1998	US BO (in $mil)	Studio
There's Something About Mary	$176.50	Fox
A Bug's Life	$162.80	Buena Vista
The Waterboy	$161.50	Buena Vista
Doctor Dolittle	$144.20	Fox
Rush Hour	$141.20	New Line
Patch Adams	$135.00	Universal
Lethal Weapon 4	$129.80	Warner Bros.
The Truman Show	$125.60	Paramount
Mulan	$120.60	Buena Vista
You've Got Mail	$115.80	Warner Bros.

Top 10 Comedies of 1999	US BO (in $mil)	Studio
Toy Story 2	$245.00	Buena Vista
Austin Powers : The Spy Who Shagged Me	$205.50	New Line
Big Daddy	$163.50	Sony
Runaway Bride	$152.20	Paramount
Stuart Little	$141.00	Sony
American Beauty	$135.00	DreamWorks
Notting Hill	$116.10	Universal
Wild Wild West	$113.80	Warner Bros.
Analyze This	$106.80	Warner Bros.
American Pie	$101.80	Universal

Top 10 Comedies of 2000	US BO (in $mil)	Studio
How The Grinch Stole Christmas	$261.00	Universal
What Women Want	$180.00	Paramount
Meet the Parents	$165.00	Universal
Scary Movie	$157.00	Miramax
Nutty Professor II : The Klumps	$123.30	Universal
Big Momma's House	$117.60	Fox
Miss Congeniality	$110.00	Warner Bros.
Chicken Run	$106.80	DreamWorks
Me, Myself, and Irene	$90.60	Fox
The Emperor's New Groove	$90.00	Buena Vista

Top 10 Comedies of 2001	US BO (in $mil)	Studio
Shrek	$267.70	DreamWorks
Monsters, Inc.	$255.00	Buena Vista
Rush Hour 2	$226.20	New Line
Ocean's Eleven	$183.40	Warner Bros.
American Pie 2	$145.10	Universal
Dr. Dolittle 2	$113.00	Fox
Spy Kids	$112.70	Miramax
The Princess Diaries	$108.20	Buena Vista
Legally Blonde	$100.60	Paramount
America's Sweethearts	$96.50	Miramax

ABOUT THE AUTHORS

Stuart Voytilla is co-founder, writer, and producer for Redfield Arts, a motion picture production company based in Baltimore, Maryland. Stuart also lectures about myth and genre, and teaches screenwriting and film aesthetics at San Diego State University. His acclaimed book on story structure and genre, *Myth and the Movies*, is published by Michael Wiese Productions. Stuart makes his home in San Diego with his wife, Barbara Rinaldo, and their daughter, Elena. For further information about his consultation service and lecture series, contact him through Michael Wiese Productions or at *www.redfieldarts.com*.

Scott Petri is an award-winning humorist and the author of 12 screenplays. Scott currently works for Walt Disney Imagineering, Research and Development. He also consults on screenplays and writes jokes for corporate clients by referral only. Scott resides in Los Angeles, California with his lovely wife, Sheila. He can be contacted at *www.shortangryman.com*.

MYTH AND THE MOVIES
Discovering the Mythic Structure of 50 Unforgettable Films

Stuart Voytilla
Foreword by Christopher Vogler, author of *The Writer's Journey*

An illuminating companion piece to *The Writer's Journey*, *Myth and the Movies* applies the mythic structure Vogler developed to 50 well-loved U.S. and foreign films. This comprehensive book offers a greater understanding of why some films continue to touch and connect with audiences generation after generation.

Movies discussed include *Die Hard*, *Singin' in the Rain*, *Boyz N the Hood*, *Pulp Fiction*, *The Searchers*, *La Strada*, and *The Silence of the Lambs*.

Stuart Voytilla is a writer, script consultant, and teacher of acting and screenwriting and the co-author of *Writing the Comedy Film*.

$26.95, 300 pages
Order # 39RLS | ISBN: 0-941188-66-3

THE WRITER'S PARTNER
1001 Breakthrough Ideas to Stimulate Your Imagination

Martin Roth

This book is the complete source, as reliable and indispensable as its title implies. Whether you're looking for inspiration for new plotlines and characters or need help fleshing out your characters and settings with depth, detail, color, and texture, Martin Roth will turn your script into a strong, memorable work. This comprehensive classic covers every major genre, from action to suspense to comedy to romance to horror. With *The Writer's Partner*, you'll feel like you're in a roomful of talented writers helping you to perfect your screenplay!

Martin Roth is the writer of *The Crime Writer's Reference Book*.

$19.95, 349 pages
Order # 3RLS | ISBN: 0-941188-32-9

WRITING THE THRILLER FILM
The Terror Within

Neill D. Hicks

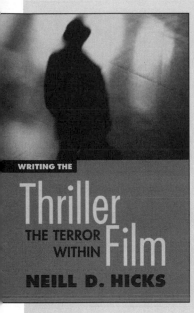

A good Thriller will rupture the reality of your everyday world. It will put you on guard. Make you *aware*. That is the disquieting objective — successfully achieved — of this book as well.

Writing the Thriller Film concentrates on the Cosmos of Credibility, those not-so-obvious elements of screenwriting that contribute the essential meaning to a script. To do so, this book traces the thematic commonalities that actually define the genre, and offers corroboration from a number of screenplays, including such classics as *North by Northwest*, *Marathon Man*, and *3 Days of the Condor*.

You will discover:
- The effect of the practical rules and physical expectations of the real world on the story
- The Timescape of the genre
- How both the protagonist and the antagonist must react to make a Thriller effective
- The need for your characters to make difficult choices with unexpected results

"Writing powerful, compelling, edge-of-the-seat movies is only one of the things Neill D. Hicks does well. Another is passing his know-how, valuable experience, and insight on to whoever is savvy enough to want to know how to structure dynamic, exciting films for the global market."
— Gloria Stern, Author
Do The Write Thing: Making the Transition To Professional

Neill D. Hicks is the author of *Writing the Action-Adventure Film* and *Screenwriting 101*.

$14.95, 168 pages
Order # 101RLS | ISBN: 0-941188-46-9 | **Available October 2002**

WRITING THE ACTION-ADVENTURE FILM
The Moment of Truth

Neill D. Hicks

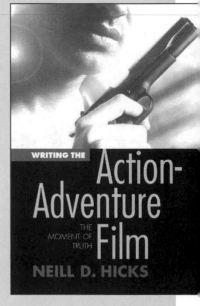

The Action-Adventure movie is consistently one of the most popular exports of the American film industry, drawing enormous audiences worldwide across many diverse societies, cultures, and languages.

But there are more than hot pursuits, hot lead, and hotheaded slugfests in a successful Action-Adventure script. With definitive examples from over 100 movies, *Writing the Action-Adventure Film* reveals the screenwriting principles that define the content and the style of this popular film genre. Neill Hicks furnishes a set of tools to build a compelling screenplay that fulfills the expectations of the motion picture audience.

You will discover how to create the Moment of Truth where the stakes are life and death, perfect a story structure that compels your characters to take immediate action, recognize the different forms of action and where to use them effectively, and develop the narrative context of adventure to surround the audience in the special world of the story.

"Dreaming about writing the next *The Matrix*, *Gladiator*, *The One*, or *Spy Game*? Neill clearly knows the Action-Adventure genre inside and out. I recommend the book highly!"
— Eric Lilleør
Publisher/Editor-in-Chief
Screentalk Magazine

Neill D. Hicks, the author of the best-selling *Screenwriting 101: The Essential Craft of Feature Film Writing* (see page 21) and *Writing the Thriller Film: The Terror Within* (see page 8), is an L.A.-based professional screenwriter whose credits include two of the biggest Action-Adventure films of all time, *Rumble in the Bronx* and *First Strike*.

$14.95, 180 pages
Order # 99RLS
ISBN: 0-941188-39-6

SCRIPT PARTNERS
What Makes Film and TV Writing Teams Work

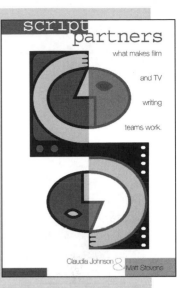

Claudia Johnson & Matt Stevens
Foreword by Marshall Brickman

Many of the most important and successful films and television shows of the past and the present have been written by script partners, from Billy Wilder's legendary collaborations with Charles Brackett and I.A.L. Diamond to the Coen Brothers' collaboration today; yet, no serious study exists of this unique and important process. Of the more than two hundred books about screenplay and television writing available today, not one focuses on collaborative writing.

This book brings together the experience, knowledge, techniques, and wisdom of many of our most successful writing teams for film and television. It examines the role and the importance of collaboration, then illuminates the process of collaborative screenwriting itself: its unique assets, from the partners' complementary strengths to the mysterious but often-mentioned "third voice" that occurs during collaborative writing; why and how they choose each other; the myriad ways that different teams work; how teams create their ideas, choose projects, develop character, story, and structure, write scenes, dialogue, draft the screenplay, rewrite, and how they manage and maintain their creative relationship. At its deepest level, that's what collaborative screenwriting is about: human relationships.

Includes interviews with such successful collaborators as Andrew Reich & Ted Cohen (*Friends*), Jim Taylor (*Election, About Schmidt*), Marshall Brickman (*Annie Hall, Manhattan*), Scott Alexander & Larry Karaszewski (*The People vs. Larry Flynt, Ed Wood*), and Larry Gelbart (*M*A*S*H*).

Claudia Johnson is the author of *Stifled Laughter*, nominated for the Pulitzer Prize, and *Crafting Short Screenplays That Connect*. Matt Stevens is a Los Angeles-based writer/producer who has sold both fiction and documentary projects. Two of their co-written scripts were recent finalists for the Sundance Screenwriters Lab.

$22.95, 300 pages
Order # 104RLS | ISBN: 0-941188-75-2 | **Available February 2003**

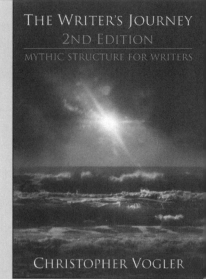

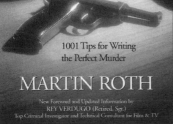

SCREENWRITING 101
The Essential Craft of Feature Film Writing

Neill D. Hicks

Hicks brings the clarity and practical instruction familiar to his students and readers to screenwriters everywhere. In his inimitable and colorful style, he tells the beginning screenwriter how the mechanics of Hollywood storytelling work, and how to use those elements to create a script with blockbuster potential without falling into clichés.

$16.95, 220 pages | Order # 41RLS | ISBN: 0-941188-72-8

SCREENWRITING ON THE INTERNET
Researching, Writing and Selling Your Script on the Web

Christopher Wehner

The Internet can save you loads of money, time, and effort — but only if you know how to exploit it. This book is your road map to using the information superhighway to further your screenwriting career. Packed with time- and money-saving tips, it includes a definitive directory and much more.

$16.95, 235 pages | Order # 5RLS | ISBN: 0-941188-36-1

FADE IN:
The Screenwriting Process, 2nd Edition

Robert A. Berman

With this concise step-by-step roadmap for developing a story concept into a finished screenplay, you will learn how to: read a screenplay; analyze a script; create three-dimensional characters; structure your story; structure your screenplay; research effectively; format professionally; use the correct terms and techniques; write the first draft; rewrite and polish until you have a final draft you are proud to submit.

$24.95, 385 Pages | Order # 30RLS | ISBN: 0-941188-58-2

THE SCRIPT-SELLING GAME
A Hollywood Insider's Look at Getting Your Script Sold and Produced

Kathie Fong Yoneda

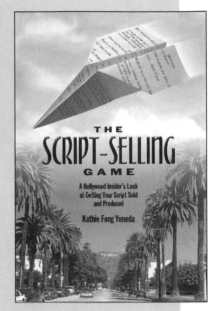

There are really only two types of people in Hollywood: those who sit around wearing black clothes in smoky coffee shops, complaining they can't get their scripts past the studio gates... and then there are the players. The ones with the hot scripts. The ones crackling with energy. The ones with knowledge.

Players understand that their success in Hollywood is not based on luck or nepotism; it's the result of understanding how Hollywood really works.

The Script-Selling Game brings together over 25 years of experience from an entertainment professional who shows you how to prepare your script, pitch it, meet the moguls, talk the talk, and make the deal. It's a must for both novice and veteran screenwriters.

"Super-concise, systematic, real-world advice on the practical aspects of screenwriting and mastering Hollywood from a professional. This book will save you time, embarrassment, and frustration and will give you an extra edge in taking on the studio system."
>   — Christopher Vogler, Author, *The Writer's Journey: Mythic Structure for Writers*, Seminar Leader, former Story Consultant with Fox 2000

"I've been extremely fortunate to have Kathie's insightful advice and constructive criticism on my screenplays. She has been a valued mentor to me. Now, through this wonderful book, she can be your mentor, as well."
>   — Pamela Wallace, Academy Award Co-Winner, Best Writing, Screenplay Written Directly for the Screen, *Witness*

Kathie Fong Yoneda is an industry veteran, currently under contract to Paramount TV in their Longform Division, and an independent script consultant whose clientele includes several award-winning writers. Kathie also conducts workshops based on *The Script-Selling Game* in the U.S. and Europe.

$14.95, 196 pages | Order # 100RLS | ISBN: 0-941188-44-2

WRITING THE KILLER TREATMENT
Selling Your Story without a Script

Michael Halperin

The most commonly heard phrase in Hollywood is not "Let's do lunch." In reality, the expression you'll most often hear in production, studio, and agency offices is: "Okay, send me a treatment."

A treatment, which may range from one to several dozen pages, is the snapshot of your feature film or TV script. A treatment reveals your story's structure, introduces your characters and hooks, and is often your first and only opportunity to pitch your project.

This is the only book that takes you through the complete process of creating treatments that sell. It includes: developing believable characters and story structure; understanding the distinctions between treatments for screenplays, adaptations, sitcoms, Movies of the Week, episodic television, and soaps; useful exercises that will help you develop your craft as a writer; insightful interviews with Oscar and Emmy winners; tips and query letters for finding an agent and/or a producer; and What Every Writer Needs to Know, from the Writers Guild of America, west.

"Michael Halperin's well-crafted book offers a meticulous – and simple – plan for writing your treatment, from its inception to the final polish."
— Sable Jak, Scr(i)pt Magazine

Michael Halperin worked as an Executive Story Consultant for 20th Century Fox Television and on staff with Universal Television. He has written and/or produced numerous television episodes. He is the author of Writing the Second Act: Building Conflict and Tension in Your Film Script.

$14.95, 171 pages
Order # 97RLS
ISBN: 0-941188-40-X

SETTING UP YOUR SHOTS
Great Camera Moves Every Filmmaker Should Know

Jeremy Vineyard

Written in straightforward, non-technical language and laid out in a nonlinear format with self-contained chapters for quick, on-the-set reference, *Setting Up Your Shots* is like a Swiss army knife for filmmakers! Using examples from over 140 popular films, this book provides detailed descriptions of more than 100 camera setups, angles, and techniques — in an easy-to-use horizontal "wide-screen" format.

Setting Up Your Shots is an excellent primer for beginning filmmakers and students of film theory, as well as a handy guide for working filmmakers. If you are a director, a storyboard artist, or an animator, use this book. It is the culmination of hundreds of hours of research.

Contains 150 references to the great shots from your favorite films, including *2001: A Space Odyssey, Blue Velvet, The Matrix, The Usual Suspects,* and *Vertigo.*

"Perfect for any film enthusiast looking for the secrets behind creating film. Because of its simplicity of design and straightforward storyboards, *Setting Up Your Shots* is destined to be mandatory reading at film schools throughout the world."
— Ross Otterman, *Directed By Magazine*

Jeremy Vineyard is a director and screenwriter who moved to Los Angeles in 1997 to pursue a feature filmmaking career. He has several spec scripts in development.

$19.95, 132 pages
Order # 8RLS
ISBN: 0-941188-73-6

MICHAEL WIESE PRODUCTIONS
11288 Ventura Blvd., Suite 621
Studio City, CA 91604
1-818-379-8799
mwpsales@mwp.com
www.mwp.com

> Write or Fax
> for a
> free catalog.

Please send me the following
books:

Title	Order Number (#RLS___)	Amount
_____	_____	
_____	_____	
_____	_____	
_____	_____	

SHIPPING _____

California Tax (8.00%) _____

TOTAL ENCLOSED _____

Please make check or money order payable to
Michael Wiese Productions

(Check one) ___ Master Card ___ Visa ___ Amex

Credit Card Number_____

Expiration Date_____

Cardholder's Name_____

Cardholder's Signature_____

SHIP TO:

Name_____

Address_____

City_____State_____Zip_____

Order online for the lowest prices at
www.mwp.com